KETO DESSERTS

KETO DESSERTS

13-Digit ISBN: 978-1-64643-041-3

10-Digit ISBN: 1-64643-041-7

This book may be ordered by mail from the publisher. Please include $5.99 for postage and handling.
Please support your local bookseller first!

Books published by Cider Mill Press Book Publishers are available at special discounts for bulk purchases in the United States by corporations, institutions, and other organizations. For more information, please contact the publisher.

Cider Mill Press Book Publishers
"Where good books are ready for press"
PO Box 454
12 Spring Street
Kennebunkport, Maine 04046
Visit us online!
www.cidermillpress.com

Typography: Adobe Garamond Pro, Gotham, Blackjack, Type Embellishments One

Image credits: Pages 18, 21, 22, 25, 26, 54, 66, 133, 137, 213, 214, 222, 225, and 238 courtesy of Cider Mill Press Book Publishers. All other images used under official license from StockFood and Shutterstock.
Front cover image: No-Bake Blueberry Cheesecake, see page 48
Back cover image: Dark Chocolate & Stout Brownies, see page 110
Front endpaper image: Chocolate Ice Cream, see page 157
Back endpaper image: Berry Cheesecake Tarts, see page 143

Printed in China

1 2 3 4 5 6 7 8 9 0

First Edition

KETO DESSERTS

Over 100 Decadent Desserts for the Keto Diet

CIDER MILL PRESS

BOOK
PUBLISHERS
KENNEBUNKPORT, MAINE

TABLE *of* CONTENTS

❋ ❋ ❋

INTRODUCTION

❋ ❋ ❋

To many people the words diet and deprivation are synonymous, especially when it comes to desserts. Left to their own devices, many people actually think about dessert first, and then work backward to decide what should precede it. For these folks, the thought of following any plan that yanks the sweet tooth out of their mouth is unacceptable.

For them, there's some great news: it's easy to enjoy luscious desserts while strictly following a keto diet, and limiting your carb intake to less than 50 grams per day. You can enjoy fudgy brownies, indulgent custards and mousses, even a rich carrot cake.

The secret to keto desserts is swapping out ingredients such as wheat flour and traditional sweeteners that are rife with carbs. While most diets ban butter, it's a boon on the keto diet. Ditto for cream cheese, heavy cream, and any nut. These green lights mean that the fat responsible for the luscious mouth feel we crave in a dessert is present and accounted for.

It's important to keep in mind that low-carb baked goods will be similar to those made with wheat flour and sugar, but they won't be identical. There will be differences in taste and texture. But the end result can be just as satisfying.

WAVING GOODBYE TO WHEAT

The first major change in keto baking is banishing the baker's old friend—all-purpose flour—from your cabinet. And that's easier said than done. But it is necessary. The carb content in ½ cup of wheat flour is 48 grams; that's almost a whole day's allotment for someone following the ketogenic diet.

Two proteins found in wheat flour, glutenin and gliadin, form an elastic substance known as gluten when stirred with moisture to activate them. There are as many as 30 different proteins in wheat, but only these two have gluten-forming potential. When wheat flour is moistened and manipulated through stirring, beating, and kneading, these two proteins hold onto water, and then form elastic strands of gluten. If a flour has a lot of these proteins, it latches onto water faster, creating strong and springy gluten.

The magical gluten network that results serves many functions. Like a net, gluten traps and holds air bubbles. They later expand due to the gas that stems from the leavening that occurs in the oven, causing the dough or batter to rise. During baking, the gluten becomes rigid as the moisture evaporates, providing the baked good with structure. The properties of gluten provide the perfect combination of elasticity and rigidity by expanding with the gas while still holding its shape. No other grain has been able to replicate this in baking.

Because of that, gluten-free and low-carb baked goods tend to be a bit denser than the standard offerings, due to the alternative flours used. So, don't be nervous if a keto-compliant recipe is calling for more baking powder or baking soda than you're accustomed to—they need a bit more of a boost to provide structure.

ALTERNATIVES TO CUT THE CARBS

When entering the world of keto desserts, there are a lot of ingredients that might be new to you. But they are easy to understand. What's important is to remember that they cannot be substituted for wheat flour on a 1-to-1 basis. The composition of every dry ingredient determines how it functions in a batter or dough.

The keto baker's best friend is almond flour, which is simply finely ground blanched almonds that have briefly been cooked. A ½ cup of almond flour contains about 12 grams of total carbohydrates, but 6 of those grams are fiber. That means the net carb count is a mere 6 grams, compared with the staggering 48 grams for wheat flour. While made from almonds, it barely tastes like almonds, and is almost pure white—the same color as unbleached, all-purpose wheat flour.

Almond flour is becoming used more frequently in conventional baking because it is the structural component of French macarons, which have skyrocketed in popularity during the past decade.

Almond flour should not be confused with, nor used interchangeably with its fraternal twin—almond meal. Almond meal is more coarsely ground, and is made from raw almonds that have not been skinned, so the color is a medium shade of brown. It will deliver a grainier product than using almond flour, and it does have some underlying almond flavor. But almond flour vs. almond meal is not a battle. Ultimately, it's a matter of personal preference.

Both hazelnuts and walnuts are also commonly ground to a flour-like consistency, and they deliver the flavors of their source nut well. They can be substituted for almond flour or meal in any recipe, should you want to introduce that flavor. Hazelnut flour is a real treat, and can now be purchased at a number of online sites.

The other frequently cited wheat flour alternative in keto desserts is coconut flour. Coconut flour is actually a by-product of coconut milk. To make the milk, producers first have to soak the coconut's meat; this is then processed and pressed to remove the liquid. The remaining pulp is then ground, and the fat removed, to make the flour drier.

You'll find that recipes using coconut flour call for very little of it; that's not a mistake. It's used at a ratio of about 1 part coconut flour to 3 or 4 parts wheat flour, as the former is super-absorbent. That's why you'll see a lot of liquid in those recipes containing it. Coconut flour is rich in vitamins and minerals, including manganese, calcium, selenium, and potassium.

There are lesser-known substitutions for wheat flour in keto baked goods, and like coconut flour, none of these contain nuts. If you want a sesame flavor and aroma in baked goods, go for sesame flour. You can make it yourself by grinding sesame seeds in a blender or spice grinder. Also in the seed-flour family is sunflower seed flour, which can be substituted 1-to-1 for almond flour.

A downside of sunflower seed flour is that it tends to turn a rather unattractive, olive green shade when it reacts with baking powder or baking soda in a recipe. To mitigate this reaction, add 1 tablespoon of apple cider vinegar or lemon juice to the recipe.

The final contender for keto baking is golden flaxseed meal, which is simply flaxseeds ground very fine. While regular flaxseed meal is a common ingredient in vegan recipes, it creates a gummy texture in baked goods. That's why the golden flaxseed meal is specified.

HOW TO SWEETEN DESSERTS WITHOUT SUGAR

The goal of the keto diet is to reach the metabolic state of ketosis, where your body begins to break down fat stores in the liver to produce energy rather than wresting it from easily accessible carbs. There are many products on the market to help you shun sugar while still enjoying luscious desserts. Most of them are natural, although their names may be difficult to spell and pronounce. Then there are the artificial ones that were born in chemistry labs rather than in nature.

One popular natural choice for sugar replacement in keto desserts is erythritol (pronounced err-ITH-rah-toll) a type of sugar alcohol. Erythritol is created when a type of yeast ferments glucose from corn or wheat starch. Most sugar alcohols are found in small amounts in nature, especially in fruits and vegetables. The way the molecules are structured gives them the ability to stimulate the sweet taste receptors on the tongue. Or, they fool the tongue into transmitting the news to the brain that something is sweet.

Granulated sugar contains 4 calories per gram, while erythritol is a mere ½ calorie per gram. Yet it contains more than 70 percent of the sweetness of sugar. Erythritol is also great for baking because it is produced in both granulated and powdered forms. If you have granulated erythritol and a recipe calls for powdered you can replicate it yourself. Simply place the granulated product in a blender (or, for small quantities, a spice grinder) and blend it to a finer texture.

A first cousin of erythritol is another sugar alcohol, xylitol. It's rarely used in cooking or baking, but is an excellent source of sweetness in beverages.

The main rival to erythritol, and the primary sweetener called for in this book, is stevia. Stevia is a natural sweetener derived from the Stevia rebaudiana plant. It contains almost no calories or carbs, and some studies have shown that it may help lower blood sugar levels. It is much sweeter than sugar, and you'll need only 1 teaspoon of pure stevia to substitute for 1 cup of granulated sugar.

Stevia is a tropical plant that is native to South America, and it's sometimes called candyleaf or sugarleaf. The Guaraní people in Brazil have used it for centuries to sweeten yerba mate tea, and also as medicine. It's now possible for gardeners worldwide to grow the attractive plant; it gets to be about 1 to 2 feet tall with bright green leaves and scentless white flowers.

A more exotic member of the natural sugar replacement family is monk fruit sweetener, made from a plant native to southern China. It contains natural sugars and antioxidants and the extract contains neither calories nor carbs. Be sure to check the package carefully because—depending on the brand and producer—the monk fruit is sometimes blended with sugar or molasses, which radically changes its ability to comply with a keto diet.

Then, of course, there are artificial products. The most popular one is sucralose, best known by the brand name Splenda. Sucralose claims to not create the same bitter aftertaste as other artificial sweeteners, and the pure product is 600 times sweeter than sugar. While sucralose is calorie-free, it's blended with dextrose, a simple sugar made from corn, and maltodextrin, made from vegetable starch, in Splenda. Each packet contains 3 calories and 1 gram of carbs.

SECRET CARB CACHES

Now that you see the large range of options available for sweetening keto-compliant desserts, the ones to avoid take names and forms beyond the word "sugar."

Maltodextrin is a highly processed sweetener made from plants like rice and corn, and it contains the same amounts of calories and carbs as sugar. While honey contains some valuable antioxidants and nutrients, it, too, is just like sugar in terms of calories and carbs. The same can be said for maple syrup, although it does contain minerals like manganese and zinc.

Fructose is the culprit that lands agave nectar on the no-fly list, and the same is true for coconut sugar. And the last warning goes to dried dates, which are very high in carbs.

PROVIDING BAKED GOODS WITH MOISTURE

The remaining ingredients that go into keto desserts will be familiar friends like eggs, dairy products, and butter. The mouth feel of food is delivered by fat more than any other component, and luckily there's virtually no limit on the fats available. What keto cooks are after is limiting carbs, and it turns out that dairy products that are higher in fat are lower in carbs.

For example, both sour cream and heavy cream only contain 0.5 grams of carbs per tablespoon. And cream cheese, a luscious addition to both sweet and savory preparations, is only 1.2 grams per tablespoon.

One suggestion: avoid softening cream cheese or butter in the microwave. Even though it's fine to melt your butter with the microwave at medium, it does change the structure of foods.

The carb content of cow's milk increases as the fat decreases. That ties to the percentage of butterfat; whole butter contains a mere 0.1 grams per tablespoon and clarified butter is a magnificent 0.0 on the carb scale. While whole milk has 12 grams of carbs per cup, that figure rises to 14 grams per cup in skim milk. If a recipe calls for milk, you'll save carbs if you use a combination of heavy cream thinned with water.

Eggs, a protein-rich ingredient that is virtually a carb-free food, are very important in low-carb baking. Most recipes rely on eggs as the key binding agent that creates the structure provided by the gluten contained in wheat flour. Eggs add moisture as well, and prevent baked goods from becoming crumbly.

Eggs also serve as a leavening agent. The whites are what create the airy texture of angel food cake, or harden into the delicate character of a meringue cookie. When using whole eggs, the fat from the yolks prevents the whites from gaining volume. The other way that eggs lighten baked goods is through the creation of steam when the liquid is heated in the oven. The eggs also trap moisture in baked goods, keeping them from becoming stale too quickly.

Egg white is very high in protein, with almost no fat, and virtually no cholesterol. It has merely 13 percent of the calories of a whole egg. The other nutrient in egg white is B-2, or riboflavin.

Coconut cream delivers fat, moisture, and coconut flavor in recipes. While it is occasionally found on store shelves, most cooks create it themselves, as it is very easy. To do so, place a can of full-fat coconut milk in the refrigerator. Once chilled, open it with a can opener without shaking. Once the lid has been removed, you'll find a thick layer of coconut cream at the top.

Some careful reading is required to select the correct baking powder for keto-friendly cooking. All baking powder is a blend of three simple ingredients: baking soda, cream of tartar, and starch. The problem lies in the starch, which can add unwanted carbs. The amount of carbs varies greatly from brand to brand. Look for a brand that only contains 1 gram of carbs per ¼ teaspoon.

GENERAL TIPS FOR SUCCESS

There are a few general guidelines that are more appropriate for keto-friendly recipes.

The first is to allow your chilled ingredients to reach room temperature so they blend together without fuss. You'll find cream cheese in many recipes, as well as butter. Both should be kept at room temperature for about 30 minutes before using.

Prepping your pan is another key to success. Keto-compliant recipes tend to create sticky and stiff doughs and batters. Follow any instructions that call for you to line the pan with parchment paper, or grease it with butter or nonstick cooking spray.

You'll notice that many recipes tell you to leave ketofied baked goods in or on their pans until they are completely cool. The reason is that these gluten-free flour alternatives do not create a structure when still hot from the oven. If you remove baked goods from pans too soon, you may find you have a collection of crumbs instead of cookies.

Do look carefully at keto recipes before starting to prepare them, because they may call for specific items. For example, high-quality chocolate is used often. But the key is to note whether the chocolate is 85 percent or 90 percent cocoa, or sugar-free.

Peanut butter is a great keto-friendly ingredient, but it, too, should be unsweetened. That's why the recipes that follow call for natural, no sugar added peanut butter.

Measuring the alternative to wheat flour also requires a different procedure. In conventional baking we're taught to scoop out the flour and level off any excess. For keto-compliant flours, take them by the heaping tablespoon and gently add them to a measuring cup.

There's no reason why watching carbs should be painful. As you can see, you'll always get your "just desserts."

※ ※ ※

CHAPTER 1

CAKES

Thanks to the versatile abilities of almond flour and the luscious mouth feel provided by keto stalwarts like heavy cream and eggs, the rightful holder of the dessert crown—the cake—is always within reach. From quick, one-serving cakes that leverage the power of the microwave to light, lemon-tinged treats and luxurious cheese cakes, there's no shortage of rich goodies in this collection.

Almond Flour Mug Cake

YIELD: **1 SERVING**
PREP TIME: **2 MINUTES**
COOKING TIME: **5 MINUTES**

NUTRITIONAL INFO:
(PER SERVING OF CAKE)
CALORIES: **395**
NET CARBS: **4 G**
CARBS: **11 G**
FAT: **36 G**
PROTEIN: **12 G**
FIBER: **7 G**

(PER SERVING OF GANACHE)
CALORIES: **125**
NET CARBS: **2 G**
CARBS: **3 G**
FAT: **18 G**
PROTEIN: **1 G**
FIBER: **1 G**

INGREDIENTS

FOR THE MUG CAKE

1 TEASPOON UNSALTED BUTTER

1 TEASPOON HEAVY CREAM

1 EGG

¼ TEASPOON PURE VANILLA EXTRACT

0.8 OZ. ALMOND FLOUR

2 TEASPOONS UNSWEETENED COCOA POWDER

PINCH OF KOSHER SALT

STEVIA OR PREFERRED KETO-FRIENDLY SWEETENER, TO TASTE

SLICED STRAWBERRIES, FOR TOPPING (OPTIONAL)

FOR THE GANACHE

½ OZ. 85 PERCENT OR HIGHER DARK CHOCOLATE, CHOPPED

2 TEASPOONS UNSALTED BUTTER

1 TEASPOON HEAVY CREAM

STEVIA OR PREFERRED KETO-FRIENDLY SWEETENER, TO TASTE

DIRECTIONS

1. To prepare the cake, place the butter, cream, egg, and vanilla in a mug and stir to combine. Add the almond flour, cocoa powder, salt, and sweetener and stir until thoroughly combined. Place the mug in the microwave and microwave on high for 1 minute. Remove, turn the mug over, and tap it until the cake slides out.

2. To prepare the ganache, place the chocolate and butter in a small bowl and microwave on high for 20 seconds. Remove, stir in the cream and sweetener, and drizzle over the cake. Top with strawberries, if desired, and serve.

Coconut Flour Mug Cake

YIELD: **1 SERVING**
PREP TIME: **5 MINUTES**
COOKING TIME: **5 MINUTES**

NUTRITIONAL INFO:
(PER SERVING OF CAKE)
CALORIES: **218**
NET CARBS: **3 G**
CARBS: **8 G**
FAT: **17 G**
PROTEIN: **5 G**
FIBER: **5 G**

(PER SERVING OF GANACHE)
CALORIES: **156**
NET CARBS: **1 G**
CARBS: **3 G**
FAT: **21 G**
PROTEIN: **3 G**
FIBER: **2 G**

INGREDIENTS

FOR THE CAKE

1 OZ. COCONUT FLOUR

2 TABLESPOONS UNSALTED BUTTER

2 TEASPOONS COCONUT MILK

½ TEASPOON PURE VANILLA EXTRACT

¼ TEASPOON BAKING POWDER

1 EGG

STEVIA OR PREFERRED KETO-FRIENDLY SWEETENER, TO TASTE

PINCH OF KOSHER SALT

FOR THE GANACHE

1½ TEASPOONS UNSALTED BUTTER OR COCOA BUTTER

1½ TEASPOONS NATURAL, NO SUGAR ADDED PEANUT BUTTER

½ TEASPOON UNSWEETENED COCOA POWDER

STEVIA, TO TASTE

½ TEASPOON COCONUT MILK

DIRECTIONS

1. To prepare the cake, combine all of the ingredients in a mug, place it in the microwave, and microwave on high for 1½ minutes. Remove, turn the mug over, and tap it until the cake falls out.

2. To prepare the ganache, place the butter and peanut butter in a bowl and microwave for 1 minute. Remove and stir to combine. Stir in the cocoa powder, sweetener, and coconut milk, and stir until thoroughly combined. Drizzle over the cake and serve.

Berry Mug Cake

YIELD: **1 SERVING**
PREP TIME: **5 MINUTES**
COOKING TIME: **15 MINUTES**

NUTRITIONAL INFO:
(PER SERVING)
CALORIES: **627**
NET CARBS: **10 G**
CARBS: **15 G**
FAT: **55 G**
PROTEIN: **12 G**
FIBER: **5 G**

INGREDIENTS

FOR THE BERRY COMPOTE

3½ OZ. BLACKBERRIES, PUREED AND STRAINED

3½ OZ. RASPBERRIES, PUREED AND STRAINED

2 TEASPOONS POWDERED ERYTHRITOL

FOR THE FROSTING

0.8 OZ. MASCARPONE CHEESE, AT ROOM TEMPERATURE

0.8 OZ. HEAVY CREAM

¼ TEASPOON PURE VANILLA EXTRACT

STEVIA OR PREFERRED KETO-FRIENDLY SWEETENER, TO TASTE

FOR THE CAKE

1 TEASPOON COCONUT FLOUR

½ TEASPOON BAKING POWDER

2 TEASPOONS BERRY COMPOTE

1 TEASPOON HEAVY CREAM

2 TEASPOONS UNSALTED BUTTER

STEVIA OR PREFERRED KETO-FRIENDLY SWEETENER, TO TASTE

1 EGG

DIRECTIONS

1. To prepare the berry compote, place all of the ingredients in a saucepan and cook over low heat, stirring occasionally, until the mixture is the consistency of jam. Remove the pan from heat and let the compote cool.

2. To prepare the frosting, place all of the ingredients in a mixing bowl and beat until the mixture is thoroughly combined and has the desired consistency. Pour the mixture into a piping bag and chill until ready to use.

3. To prepare the cake, place all of the ingredients in a mug or ramekin and whisk until combined. Microwave on high for 2½ to 3 minutes, until a toothpick inserted into the center comes out clean. Top with the frosting and remaining compote and serve immediately.

Peanut Butter Mug Cake

YIELD: **1 SERVING**

PREP TIME: **2 MINUTES**

COOKING TIME: **2 MINUTES**

NUTRITIONAL INFO:

(PER SERVING WITHOUT WHIPPED CREAM)

CALORIES: **533**

NET CARBS: **9 G**

CARBS: **16 G**

FAT: **47 G**

PROTEIN: **21 G**

FIBER: **7 G**

INGREDIENTS

2.1 OZ. NATURAL, NO SUGAR ADDED PEANUT BUTTER

2 TEASPOONS UNSWEETENED COCOA POWDER

1 TEASPOON UNSALTED BUTTER, MELTED

1 EGG

1 TEASPOON HEAVY CREAM

½ TEASPOON BAKING POWDER

STEVIA OR PREFERRED KETO-FRIENDLY SWEETENER, TO TASTE

WHIPPED CREAM (SEE PAGE 238), FOR GARNISH (OPTIONAL)

DIRECTIONS

1. Place all of the ingredients, other than the Whipped Cream (if using), in a mug and whisk until smooth.

2. Microwave for 1 minute and top with Whipped Cream, if desired.

Coffee Cakes

YIELD: **2 SERVINGS**
PREP TIME: **5 MINUTES**
COOKING TIME: **5 MINUTES**

NUTRITIONAL INFO:
(PER SERVING)
CALORIES: **294**
NET CARBS: **3 G**
CARBS: **5 G**
FAT: **28 G**
PROTEIN: **7 G**
FIBER: **2 G**

INGREDIENTS

FOR THE CAKES

1 TABLESPOON UNSALTED BUTTER

1 OZ. HEAVY CREAM

1 TEASPOON POWDERED ERYTHRITOL

1 TEASPOON INSTANT COFFEE POWDER

½ TEASPOON PURE VANILLA EXTRACT

PINCH OF KOSHER SALT

1 EGG

½ TEASPOON BAKING POWDER

0.7 OZ. ALMOND FLOUR

2 TEASPOONS PSYLLIUM HUSK

1 TEASPOON UNSWEETENED COCOA POWDER

FOR THE FROSTING

0.8 OZ. MASCARPONE CHEESE

0.8 OZ. HEAVY CREAM

¼ TEASPOON PURE VANILLA EXTRACT

STEVIA, TO TASTE

DIRECTIONS

1. To begin preparations for the cakes, place the butter in a bowl and microwave on medium for 20 seconds, until it has melted. Stir in the cream, erythritol, and instant coffee powder. If the instant coffee does not dissolve, microwave for another 15 seconds and stir until it does.

2. Add the vanilla, salt, and egg and stir until thoroughly combined. Add the baking powder, almond flour, psyllium husk, and cocoa powder and stir until the mixture is a smooth batter. Divide the batter between two ramekins or mugs and microwave for a minute each. Remove and let cool.

3. To prepare the frosting, place all of the ingredients in a small bowl and stir until combined. Spread over the cakes and serve.

Mocha Sponge Cake

YIELD: **12 SERVINGS**
PREP TIME: **10 MINUTES**
COOKING TIME: **1 HOUR AND 10 MINUTES**

NUTRITIONAL INFO:
(PER SERVING)
CALORIES: **302**
NET CARBS: **9.3 G**
CARBS: **11.6 G**
FAT: **26.5 G**
PROTEIN: **5.1 G**
FIBER: **2.3 G**

DIRECTIONS

1. Preheat the oven to 350°F, line a springform pan with parchment paper, and grease it with cooking spray. To begin preparations for the cake, place the coffee, almond flour, flaxseed meal, coconut flour, baking powder, xanthan gum, and salt in a mixing bowl and stir to combine.

2. Place the butter, cream, and cocoa powder in a separate, heatproof bowl and place over a half-full saucepan of simmering water. Whisk until the mixture is smooth, remove from heat, and let cool for 5 minutes.

3. Stir the sweetener into the melted butter mixture and then incorporate the eggs one at a time. Add the dry mixture and stir until the batter is smooth. Pour the batter into the pan and gently tap it to distribute evenly. Place in the oven and bake, rotating the pan halfway through, for about 20 minutes, until a toothpick inserted into the center comes out clean. Remove from the oven and let cool on a wire rack. When the cake has cooled, cut the top one-third of it off and set the cakes aside.

4. To begin preparations for the frosting and topping, place the instant coffee and hot water in a small bowl and stir to combine. When the coffee has dissolved, stir the mixture into the frosting and set it aside.

5. Spread the jam on the larger cake and top with some of the frosting. Place the other cake on top, gently press down on it, and then cover the entire cake with the remaining frosting. Refrigerate the cake for 30 minutes. To serve, sprinkle the cocoa powder over the top before slicing and serving.

INGREDIENTS

FOR THE CAKE

1 TEASPOON INSTANT COFFEE

1 CUP ALMOND FLOUR

¼ CUP GOLDEN FLAXSEED MEAL

1½ TABLESPOONS COCONUT FLOUR

2 TEASPOONS BAKING POWDER

½ TEASPOON XANTHAN GUM

½ TEASPOON KOSHER SALT

1 STICK OF UNSALTED BUTTER, AT ROOM TEMPERATURE

¼ CUP HEAVY CREAM

¾ CUP UNSWEETENED COCOA POWDER

⅔ CUP STEVIA OR PREFERRED KETO-FRIENDLY SWEETENER

4 LARGE EGGS, AT ROOM TEMPERATURE

FOR THE FROSTING & TOPPING

2 TEASPOONS INSTANT COFFEE

1 TABLESPOON HOT WATER (125°F)

VANILLA BUTTERCREAM FROSTING (SEE PAGE 31)

¾ CUP SUGAR-FREE CHERRY JAM

1 TABLESPOON UNSWEETENED COCOA POWDER

Vanilla Buttercream Frosting

YIELD: **12 SERVINGS**
PREP TIME: **5 MINUTES**
COOKING TIME: **5 MINUTES**

NUTRITIONAL INFO:
(PER SERVING)
CALORIES: **89**
NET CARBS: **0.1 G**
CARBS: **0.1 G**
FAT: **9.6 G**
PROTEIN: **0 G**
FIBER: **0 G**

INGREDIENTS

11 TABLESPOONS UNSALTED
BUTTER, AT ROOM TEMPERATURE

SEEDS OF ½ VANILLA BEAN

½ TEASPOON PURE VANILLA
EXTRACT

PINCH OF KOSHER SALT

1 CUP SWERVE CONFECTIONERS'

1 TO 2 TABLESPOONS HEAVY
CREAM

DIRECTIONS

1. Beat the butter in a mixing bowl with a handheld mixer until fluffy. Add the vanilla seeds, vanilla extract, salt, and confectioners' sweetener. Stir to combine and then beat on high until smooth.

2. Stir in enough cream to achieve the desired consistency. Use immediately or store in the refrigerator, where the frosting will keep for up to 1 week.

Strawberry Sponge Cakes

YIELD: **12 SERVINGS**
PREP TIME: **5 MINUTES**
COOKING TIME: **35 MINUTES**

NUTRITIONAL INFO:
(PER SERVING)
CALORIES: **217**
NET CARBS: **8 G**
CARBS: **10.3 G**
FAT: **17.6 G**
PROTEIN: **6.7 G**
FIBER: **2.3 G**

INGREDIENTS

2¼ CUPS ALMOND FLOUR

½ CUP STEVIA OR PREFERRED KETO-FRIENDLY SWEETENER, PLUS ¼ CUP

2 TEASPOONS BAKING POWDER

PINCH OF KOSHER SALT

4 LARGE EGGS

1 STICK OF UNSALTED BUTTER, MELTED

1 TEASPOON PURE VANILLA EXTRACT

⅔ CUP SUGAR-FREE STRAWBERRY JAM, WARMED

DIRECTIONS

1. Preheat the oven to 350°F. Line two round 8-inch cake pans with parchment paper and grease the paper with nonstick cooking spray. Whisk together the almond flour, ½ cup of sweetener, baking powder, and salt. Add the eggs, butter, and vanilla and stir until the mixture is a smooth batter. Divide the batter between the pans and tap them gently to make sure it is evenly distributed.

2. Place in the oven and bake for about 20 minutes, until the cakes are dry to the touch and a toothpick inserted into their centers comes out clean. Remove and let cool completely on a wire rack.

3. Place the remaining sweetener in a food processor and pulse until fine and powdery. Set one of the cakes on a plate and spread the warmed jam over it. Place the second cake on top and gently press down on it. Sprinkle the finely ground sweetener over the cake and serve.

Bundt Cake

YIELD: **12 SERVINGS**
PREP TIME: **5 MINUTES**
COOKING TIME: **40 MINUTES**

NUTRITIONAL INFO:
(PER SERVING)
CALORIES: **215**
NET CARBS: **4.4 G**
CARBS: **6.4 G**
FAT: **18.9 G**
PROTEIN: **7 G**
FIBER: **2 G**

INGREDIENTS

4 OZ. CREAM CHEESE, AT ROOM TEMPERATURE

4 TABLESPOONS UNSALTED BUTTER, AT ROOM TEMPERATURE

¾ CUP STEVIA OR PREFERRED KETO-FRIENDLY SWEETENER

1 TEASPOON PURE VANILLA EXTRACT

2 TEASPOONS LEMON ZEST

4 LARGE EGGS

¼ CUP SOUR CREAM

2 CUPS ALMOND FLOUR

2 TEASPOONS BAKING POWDER

PINCH OF KOSHER SALT

HOT WATER (125°F), AS NEEDED

DIRECTIONS

1. Preheat the oven to 350°F and grease a fluted tube pan with nonstick cooking spray. Place the cream cheese, butter, ½ cup of the sweetener, vanilla, and lemon zest in a mixing bowl and beat until pale and fluffy.

2. Incorporate the eggs one at a time, and then stir in the sour cream. Gradually add the almond flour, baking powder, and salt and fold until incorporated. Pour the batter into the pan and tap it gently to evenly distribute.

3. Place in the oven and bake for about 40 minutes, until a toothpick inserted in the center comes out clean. Remove and place on a wire rack to cool completely.

4. Place the remaining sweetener in a food processor and pulse until fine and powdery. Place it in a mixing bowl and stir in teaspoons of hot water until the mixture has the consistency of icing. Pour the icing over the cake and let it set before slicing and serving.

Chocolate Cake

YIELD: **12 SERVINGS**
PREP TIME: **5 MINUTES**
COOKING TIME: **25 MINUTES**

NUTRITIONAL INFO:
(PER SERVING)
CALORIES: **264**
NET CARBS: **4.2 G**
CARBS: **7 G**
FAT: **25.4 G**
PROTEIN: **3.1 G**
FIBER: **2.8 G**

INGREDIENTS

1 STICK OF UNSALTED BUTTER, PLUS 1 TABLESPOON, AT ROOM TEMPERATURE

¾ CUP STEVIA OR PREFERRED KETO-FRIENDLY SWEETENER

2 LARGE EGGS

½ TEASPOON PURE VANILLA EXTRACT

½ CUP ALMOND FLOUR

½ CUP COCONUT FLOUR

1 TEASPOON BAKING POWDER

6 TABLESPOONS UNSWEETENED COCOA POWDER

½ CUP MILK

½ CUP CHOCOLATE FROSTING (SEE PAGE 65)

DIRECTIONS

1. Preheat the oven to 350°F and grease a round 9-inch cake pan with the tablespoon of butter. In a large bowl, beat the remaining butter and sweetener together until the mixture is light and fluffy. Incorporate the eggs one at a time and then stir in the vanilla.

2. In a small bowl, combine the flours, baking powder, and cocoa powder. Alternate adding the flour mixture and the milk to the butter-and-sugar mixture, stirring after each addition until it has been incorporated.

3. Pour the batter into the cake pan. Put the pan in the oven and bake for about 20 to 25 minutes, until a toothpick inserted in the middle comes out clean. Remove the pan from the oven and let the cake cool completely before applying the frosting.

Lava Cakes

YIELD: **4 SERVINGS**
PREP TIME: **15 MINUTES**
COOKING TIME: **10 MINUTES**

NUTRITIONAL INFO:
(PER SERVING)
CALORIES: **152**
NET CARBS: **3.5 G**
CARBS: **7.1 G**
FAT: **11.8 G**
PROTEIN: **8.7 G**
FIBER: **3.6 G**

INGREDIENTS

VEGETABLE OIL, AS NEEDED

¼ CUP HEAVY CREAM

4 LARGE EGGS

½ TEASPOON KOSHER SALT

1 TEASPOON BAKING POWDER

1 TEASPOON PURE VANILLA
EXTRACT

½ CUP UNSWEETENED COCOA
POWDER

½ CUP GRANULATED ERYTHRITOL

DIRECTIONS

1. Preheat the oven to 350°F and grease four ramekins with vegetable oil. Place the cream, eggs, salt, baking powder, and vanilla in a bowl and whisk until combined. Stir in the cocoa powder and erythritol and divide the mixture between the ramekins.

2. Place in the oven and bake for 10 to 12 minutes, until the cakes are set. Place a plate over the top of each ramekin, invert it, and tap on a counter to release the cake. Serve immediately.

Vanilla Cake

YIELD: **8 SERVINGS**
PREP TIME: **5 MINUTES**
COOKING TIME: **35 MINUTES**

NUTRITIONAL INFO:
(PER SERVING)
CALORIES: **99**
NET CARBS: **4.1 G**
CARBS: **6.4 G**
FAT: **4.7 G**
PROTEIN: **7.4 G**
FIBER: **2.3 G**

INGREDIENTS

1 TABLESPOON UNSALTED BUTTER, AT ROOM TEMPERATURE

½ CUP COCONUT FLOUR

½ CUP ALMOND FLOUR

½ TEASPOON KOSHER SALT

12 LARGE EGG WHITES, AT ROOM TEMPERATURE

1½ TEASPOONS CREAM OF TARTAR

¾ CUP STEVIA OR PREFERRED KETO-FRIENDLY SWEETENER

1 TABLESPOON PURE VANILLA EXTRACT

DIRECTIONS

1. Preheat the oven to 350°F and grease a fluted tube pan with the butter. Place the flours and salt in a bowl and whisk to combine. Place the egg whites and cream of tartar in a separate bowl and beat until frothy, about 1 minute. Gradually add the sweetener and beat until the mixture holds soft peaks. Add the vanilla and beat until incorporated.

2. Sift the dry mixture into the egg whites and fold to incorporate. Spoon the batter into the pan.

3. Place in the oven and bake, rotating the pan halfway through, for about 35 minutes, until the cake is golden brown on top and a toothpick inserted into the center comes out clean. Remove from the oven and let the cake cool completely before slicing and serving.

CRÈME ANGLAISE

Place 1 cup heavy cream, ½ cup whole milk, and the seeds of 1 vanilla bean in a saucepan and stir to combine. Bring to a simmer over medium heat. While the mixture is warming, whisk together 4 egg yolks and ¼ cup preferred keto-friendly sweetener in a heatproof bowl until pale and thick. Gradually whisk in the cream mixture until fully incorporated. Pour the custard back into the saucepan and cook over medium-low heat until thick enough to coat the back of a spoon. Strain the custard through a sieve before using. This preparation will produce 8 servings of crème anglaise. The macros per serving are as follows: 146 calories, 2.6 grams net carbs, 2.6 grams carbs, 13.8 grams fat, 2.5 grams protein, 0 grams fiber.

Pound Cake

YIELD: **12 SERVINGS**
PREP TIME: **5 MINUTES**
COOKING TIME: **1 HOUR AND 15 MINUTES**

NUTRITIONAL INFO:
(PER SERVING)
CALORIES: **320**
NET CARBS: **6 G**
CARBS: **9.3 G**
FAT: **27.6 G**
PROTEIN: **10.9 G**
FIBER: **3.3 G**

INGREDIENTS

1 STICK OF UNSALTED BUTTER, AT ROOM TEMPERATURE

1 CUP STEVIA OR PREFERRED KETO-FRIENDLY SWEETENER

8 OZ. CREAM CHEESE, AT ROOM TEMPERATURE

8 LARGE EGGS, AT ROOM TEMPERATURE

2 TEASPOONS PURE VANILLA EXTRACT

2½ CUPS ALMOND FLOUR

½ CUP COCONUT FLOUR

½ TEASPOON KOSHER SALT

1½ TEASPOONS BAKING POWDER

DIRECTIONS

1. Preheat the oven to 350°F and grease a 9 x 5-inch loaf pan with nonstick cooking spray. Place the butter and sweetener in a mixing bowl and beat with a handheld mixer until smooth. Incorporate the cream cheese an ounce at a time, and then incorporate the eggs one at a time. Stir in the vanilla and set the mixture aside.

2. Stir together the almond flour, coconut flour, salt, and baking powder in a separate mixing bowl. Add the dry mixture to the wet mixture and stir until the mixture is a smooth batter. Pour it into the loaf pan.

3. Place in the oven and bake for about 1 hour, until the cake is dry to the touch and a toothpick inserted into the center comes out clean. Remove and let cool completely before slicing and serving. If you're looking for toppings, the Sugar Glaze on page 109 or the Crème Anglaise on the opposite page are great options.

Lemon & Poppy Seed Pound Cake

YIELD: **12 SERVINGS**
PREP TIME: **10 MINUTES**
COOKING TIME: **50 MINUTES**

NUTRITIONAL INFO:
(PER SERVING)
CALORIES: **272**
NET CARBS: **4.7 G**
CARBS: **6.9 G**
FAT: **24.9 G**
PROTEIN: **7.6 G**
FIBER: **2.2 G**

INGREDIENTS

1 STICK OF UNSALTED BUTTER, PLUS MORE AS NEEDED

2 OZ. CREAM CHEESE, AT ROOM TEMPERATURE

1 CUP SOUR CREAM

4 LARGE EGGS

ZEST OF 1 LEMON

¼ CUP FRESH LEMON JUICE

1 CUP GRANULATED ERYTHRITOL

2 TEASPOONS BAKING POWDER

PINCH OF KOSHER SALT

2 CUPS ALMOND FLOUR

2 TABLESPOONS POPPY SEEDS

½ CUP POWDERED ERYTHRITOL

DIRECTIONS

1. Preheat the oven to 350°F and place a rack in the midde position. Grease a 9 x 5-inch loaf pan or a fluted tube pan with butter. Cut the stick of butter into small cubes and place it in a microwave-safe dish. Place in the microwave and microwave on medium until the butter is melted, removing to stir every 20 seconds. Stir in the cream cheese and work the mixture until it is smooth.

2. Transfer the butter mixture into a large mixing bowl and stir in the sour cream, eggs, lemon zest, 3 tablespoons of the lemon juice, the granulated erythritol, baking powder, and salt. When the mixture is smooth, add the almond flour and poppy seeds and stir until incorporated.

3. Pour the batter into the pan, place in the oven, and bake for 50 minutes, until a toothpick inserted into the center comes out clean. Remove and let the cake cool completely on a wire rack.

4. To serve, place the powdered erythritol and remaining lemon juice in a small bowl. Stir until combined and then drizzle the glaze over the cake.

    TIP: Slices of this cake are also delicious toasted with some cream cheese spread on them.

Coffee Cheesecakes

YIELD: **4 SERVINGS**

PREP TIME: **5 MINUTES**

REFRIGERATION TIME: **4 HOURS**

NUTRITIONAL INFO:
(PER SERVING)

CALORIES: **471**

NET CARBS: **5.9 G**

CARBS: **6 G**

FAT: **47.9 G**

PROTEIN: **7.7 G**

FIBER: **0.1 G**

INGREDIENTS

FOR THE BASES

1½ TABLESPOONS FINELY GROUND COFFEE

½ CUP LIGHT CREAM

½ TABLESPOON GELATIN

2 TABLESPOONS COLD WATER

8 OZ. CREAM CHEESE, AT ROOM TEMPERATURE

2 TABLESPOONS STEVIA OR PREFERRED KETO-FRIENDLY SWEETENER

⅓ CUP HEAVY CREAM

FOR THE TOPPING

⅔ CUP HEAVY CREAM

1 TEASPOON STEVIA OR PREFERRED KETO-FRIENDLY SWEETENER

½ TEASPOON PURE VANILLA EXTRACT

½ TEASPOON FINELY GROUND COFFEE

DIRECTIONS

1. To begin preparations for the bases, place the coffee and light cream in a saucepan and warm until the mixture starts to steam. Remove from heat, cover, and let it sit for 10 minutes. Place the gelatin and water in a small bowl and let sit for 10 minutes. Place the cream cheese and sweetener in a mixing bowl and beat with a handheld mixer until fluffy.

2. Strain the coffee cream into a saucepan, add the gelatin mixture, and cook over low heat, whisking constantly, until the gelatin has dissolved. Add this mixture to the cream cheese mixture, beat until thoroughly incorporated, and let sit for 30 minutes.

3. Beat the heavy cream until soft peaks form. Working in three increments, fold the whipped heavy cream into the cream cheese mixture. Divide the mixture between four ramekins, cover with plastic wrap, and refrigerate for 4 hours.

4. To prepare the topping, place the cream, sweetener, and vanilla in a mixing bowl and beat until the mixture holds soft peaks. Spoon into a piping bag fitted with a round piping tip and pipe it over the cheesecakes. Sprinkle some coffee over the top of each cake and serve.

No-Bake Blueberry Cheesecake

YIELD: **12 SERVINGS**
PREP TIME: **5 MINUTES**
REFRIGERATION TIME: **4 HOURS**

NUTRITIONAL INFO:
(PER SERVING)
CALORIES: **213**
NET CARBS: **8.7 G**
CARBS: **10.5 G**
FAT: **16.6 G**
PROTEIN: **6.1 G**
FIBER: **1.8 G**

INGREDIENTS

3¾ OZ. RAW CASHEWS

2 OZ. UNSWEETENED SHREDDED COCONUT

2 TABLESPOONS COCONUT OIL

7 OZ. BLUEBERRIES

2 TABLESPOONS BEET JUICE

¼ CUP STEVIA OR PREFERRED KETO-FRIENDLY SWEETENER

1 TABLESPOON WATER

1 (14 OZ.) CAN OF COCONUT MILK, CHILLED

2 CUPS PLAIN GREEK YOGURT

8½ OZ. FIRM SILKEN TOFU

DIRECTIONS

1. Line a springform pan with parchment paper and grease the paper with nonstick cooking spray. Place 1 cup of the cashews, the coconut, and coconut oil in a food processor and pulse until the mixture is coarse crumbs. Press the mixture into the base of the springform pan and refrigerate.

2. Place 1⅔ cups of the blueberries, the beet juice, sweetener, and water in a saucepan, cover the pan, and cook over medium heat until the berries are soft and juicy, about 6 to 8 minutes. Transfer them to a blender and puree until smooth.

3. Working over a mixing bowl, strain the puree through a fine sieve. Add the coconut milk, yogurt, and tofu and whisk until smooth. Scrape the mixture on top of the base and refrigerate for 4 hours.

4. Crush the remaining cashews and sprinkle them on top of the cake, along with the remaining blueberries.

No-Bake Raspberry Cheesecake

YIELD: **12 SERVINGS**
PREP TIME: **10 MINUTES**
FREEZING TIME: **4 HOURS**

NUTRITIONAL INFO:
(PER SERVING)
CALORIES: **349**
NET CARBS: **8.2 G**
CARBS: **12.2 G**
FAT: **31.4 G**
PROTEIN: **8 G**
FIBER: **4 G**

INGREDIENTS

FOR THE BASE

4.2 OZ. MIXED NUTS

2 TABLESPOONS STEVIA OR
PREFERRED KETO-FRIENDLY
SWEETENER

2 TABLESPOONS ALMOND FLOUR

⅓ CUP COCONUT OIL, MELTED

FOR THE TOP LAYER

7½ OZ. RAW CASHEWS

JUICE OF 1 LARGE LEMON

⅓ CUP COCONUT OIL, MELTED

1 CUP COCONUT MILK

1 LB. SILKEN TOFU

½ CUP STEVIA OR PREFERRED
KETO-FRIENDLY SWEETENER

4 OZ. RASPBERRIES

2 TABLESPOONS CACAO NIBS,
CHOPPED, FOR GARNISH

DIRECTIONS

1. To prepare the base, preheat the oven to 350°F. Place all of the ingredients in a food processor and pulse until the mixture is coarse crumbs. Press into a greased springform pan, place in the oven, and bake for about 12 minutes, until the crust is just set. Remove and store in the refrigerator.

2. To begin preparations for the top layer, place the cashews in a mixing bowl, cover with hot water, and let them sit for 15 minutes. Drain the cashews and place them in a clean food processor with the lemon juice, coconut oil, coconut milk, tofu, and sweetener. Pulse on high until smooth and scrape two-thirds of the mixture into a bowl. Add two-thirds of the raspberries to the food processor and puree until smooth. Spoon the mixture with no raspberries over the base and top with the raspberry puree.

3. Cover with plastic wrap and freeze for 4 hours. Remove, let sit at room temperature for 10 minutes, and top with the remaining raspberries and the cacao nibs.

Coconut Cheesecake

YIELD: **12 SERVINGS**
PREP TIME: **10 MINUTES**
REFRIGERATION TIME: **24 HOURS**

NUTRITIONAL INFO:
(PER SERVING)
CALORIES: **504**
NET CARBS: **5.8 G**
CARBS: **8.2 G**
FAT: **49.1 G**
PROTEIN: **11.5 G**
FIBER: **2.4 G**

INGREDIENTS

FOR THE BASE

1½ CUPS ALMOND FLOUR

1 TEASPOON LIME ZEST

3 TABLESPOONS STEVIA OR
PREFERRED KETO-FRIENDLY
SWEETENER

1 STICK OF UNSALTED BUTTER,
MELTED

FOR THE TOP LAYER

2 LBS. CREAM CHEESE, AT ROOM
TEMPERATURE

¾ CUP STEVIA OR PREFERRED
KETO-FRIENDLY SWEETENER

¾ CUP COCONUT MILK

3 TABLESPOONS HEAVY CREAM

4 LARGE EGGS

2 TEASPOONS LIME ZEST

1 TEASPOON PURE VANILLA
EXTRACT

2 OZ. UNSWEETENED SHREDDED
COCONUT

DIRECTIONS

1. Preheat the oven to 350°F. To prepare the base, place all of the ingredients in a food processor and pulse until the mixture is coarse crumbs. Press the mixture into a greased springform pan, cover with aluminum foil, and store in the refrigerator.

2. To prepare the top layer, place all of the ingredients, except for the coconut, in a large mixing bowl and stir to combine. Beat until the mixture is thick and smooth and then spread it over the base. Sprinkle the coconut over the top.

3. Place the cheesecake in the oven and bake for 15 minutes. Reduce the oven's temperature to 300°F and bake for another 1 hour and 10 minutes, until the filling is set at the edges and the center wobbles very slightly. Remove from the oven and let cool completely on a wire rack.

4. Place the cake in the refrigerator and chill overnight.

Lemon & Ricotta Tea Cake

YIELD: **8 SERVINGS**
PREP TIME: **10 MINUTES**
COOKING TIME: **50 MINUTES**

NUTRITIONAL INFO:
(PER SERVING)
CALORIES: **194**
NET CARBS: **2 G**
CARBS: **3 G**
FAT: **18 G**
PROTEIN: **6 G**
FIBER: **1 G**

INGREDIENTS

2.8 OZ. UNSALTED BUTTER

3½ OZ. SUKRIN GOLD OR PREFERRED KETO-FRIENDLY SWEETENER

1 TEASPOON PURE VANILLA EXTRACT

3 EGGS

5⅓ OZ. RICOTTA CHEESE

ZEST AND JUICE OF 1 LEMON

3½ OZ. ALMOND FLOUR

1 TEASPOON BAKING POWDER

SLIVERED ALMONDS, FOR GARNISH

LEMON SLICES, FOR GARNISH

DIRECTIONS

1. Preheat the oven to 325°F and grease a square 8-inch cake pan with nonstick cooking spray. Place the butter, sweetener, and vanilla in a mixing bowl and beat with a handheld mixer until pale and fluffy. If using a granulated sweetener, make sure to grind it into a fine powder in the blender before using, so that it has an easier time dissolving. Incorporate the eggs one at a time and beat until frothy. Stir in the ricotta and lemon zest and juice and set the mixture aside.

2. Sift the almond flour and baking powder into a separate bowl and stir, making sure there are no lumps. Working in two batches, stir the dry mixture into the wet mixture.

3. Pour the batter into the pan and place it in the oven. Bake for about 50 minutes, until a toothpick inserted into the center comes up with only a few crumbs. Remove and let the cake cool before slicing. Garnish with slivered almonds and lemon slices before serving.

Carrot Cake

YIELD: **24 SERVINGS**
PREP TIME: **10 MINUTES**
REFRIGERATION TIME:
4 HOURS AND 30 MINUTES

NUTRITIONAL INFO:
(PER SERVING)
CALORIES: **309**
NET CARBS: **7.7 G**
CARBS: **12.1 G**
FAT: **29.5 G**
PROTEIN: **5.6 G**
FIBER: **4.4 G**

DIRECTIONS

1. Preheat the oven to 350°F, line two round 9-inch cake pans with parchment paper, and grease the paper with nonstick cooking spray. To begin preparations for the cakes, place the butter and sweetener in a large mixing bowl and beat with a handheld mixer until the mixture is fluffy. Add the vanilla and then incorporate the eggs one at a time.

2. Place the almond flour, baking powder, cinnamon, and salt in a separate mixing bowl and stir to combine. Working in three increments, incorporate the dry mixture into the wet mixture and then fold in the carrots. Divide the batter between the pans and gently tap them to evenly distribute it.

3. Place in the oven and bake for about 25 minutes, until a toothpick inserted into the centers of the cakes comes out clean. Remove and let them cool in the pans for 15 minutes before turning the cakes onto wire racks and letting them cool completely.

4. To prepare the filling, place the pecans and sweetener in a food processor and pulse until finely ground. Place the mixture in a mixing bowl, add the butter, and beat until just combined. Add the remaining ingredients and beat until the mixture is thick and smooth.

5. Place one of the cakes in a springform pan and spread the filling over the top. Place the other cake on top and press down gently on it. Cover with plastic wrap and refrigerate for 4 hours.

6. To prepare the ganache, place the chocolate and coconut oil in a heatproof bowl. Place the cream in a saucepan and warm over medium heat until it is just about to come to a boil. Pour the hot cream over the chocolate and coconut oil and let the mixture stand for 1 minute. Add the sweetener and stir until the mixture is smooth. Pour the ganache over the cake, return the cake to the refrigerator, and chill for 30 minutes before serving.

INGREDIENTS

FOR THE CAKES

1½ STICKS UNSALTED BUTTER,
AT ROOM TEMPERATURE

¾ CUP STEVIA OR PREFERRED
KETO-FRIENDLY SWEETENER

1 TEASPOON PURE VANILLA
EXTRACT

4 LARGE EGGS

2½ CUPS ALMOND FLOUR

2 TEASPOONS BAKING POWDER

2 TEASPOONS CINNAMON

½ TEASPOON KOSHER SALT

3 LARGE CARROTS, GRATED

FOR THE FILLING

2¼ OZ. PECANS

1¼ CUPS STEVIA OR PREFERRED
KETO-FRIENDLY SWEETENER

1 STICK OF UNSALTED BUTTER,
AT ROOM TEMPERATURE

8 OZ. CREAM CHEESE, AT ROOM
TEMPERATURE

3 TABLESPOONS HEAVY CREAM

2 TEASPOONS PURE VANILLA
EXTRACT

½ TEASPOON CINNAMON

FOR THE GANACHE

6¼ OZ. SUGAR-FREE SEMISWEET
CHOCOLATE CHIPS

1 TABLESPOON COCONUT OIL

¾ CUP HEAVY CREAM

STEVIA OR PREFERRED KETO-
FRIENDLY SWEETENER, TO TASTE

Berry Ricotta Cake

YIELD: **12 SERVINGS**
PREP TIME: **10 MINUTES**
REFRIGERATION TIME: **24 HOURS**

NUTRITIONAL INFO:
(PER SERVING)
CALORIES: **389**
NET CARBS: **6.6 G**
CARBS: **9.5 G**
FAT: **35.1 G**
PROTEIN: **12.7 G**
FIBER: **2.9 G**

INGREDIENTS

FOR THE BASE

2 CUPS ALMOND FLOUR

⅓ CUP COCONUT OIL, MELTED

3 TABLESPOONS STEVIA OR
PREFERRED KETO-FRIENDLY
SWEETENER

1 TEASPOON PURE VANILLA
EXTRACT

FOR THE TOP LAYER

1 CUP STEVIA OR PREFERRED
KETO-FRIENDLY SWEETENER,
PLUS 2 TABLESPOONS

1 LB. CREAM CHEESE, AT ROOM
TEMPERATURE

17 OZ. RICOTTA CHEESE, AT ROOM
TEMPERATURE

3 LARGE EGGS

1 TEASPOON PURE VANILLA
EXTRACT

4 OZ. RASPBERRIES

2 TABLESPOONS WATER

DIRECTIONS

1. Preheat the oven to 350°F, line a springform pan with parchment paper, and grease it with nonstick cooking spray. To prepare the base, place all of the ingredients in a mixing bowl and stir until the mixture is coarse crumbs. Press the mixture into the pan, place it in the oven, and bake for about 15 minutes, until golden brown and just set. Remove and let cool completely on a wire rack.

2. To begin preparations for the top layer, pulse the 1 cup of sweetener in a food processor until fine and powdery. Place it in a mixing bowl, add the cream cheese and ricotta, and beat with a handheld mixer until smooth and creamy. Incorporate the eggs one at a time and then stir in the vanilla. Spread the mixture over the base, place the cake in the oven, and bake for about 45 minutes, until the filling is set at the edges and the center gives a slight wobble. Remove and let cool completely on a wire rack. Cover with plastic wrap and refrigerate overnight.

3. Place three-quarters of the raspberries, the remaining sweetener, and the water in a food processor and puree until smooth. Strain the puree through a fine sieve and spread it on top of the cake. Distribute the remaining raspberries on top and serve.

Brownie Cheesecake

YIELD: **12 SERVINGS**
PREP TIME: **5 MINUTES**
COOKING TIME: **55 MINUTES**

NUTRITIONAL INFO:
(PER SERVING)
CALORIES: **354**
NET CARBS: **5.9 G**
CARBS: **8.1G**
FAT: **33.8 G**
PROTEIN: **7.2 G**
FIBER: **2.2 G**

INGREDIENTS

FOR THE BASE

2 STICKS OF UNSALTED BUTTER, MELTED

1¼ CUPS STEVIA OR PREFERRED KETO-FRIENDLY SWEETENER

⅔ CUP UNSWEETENED COCOA POWDER

4 LARGE EGGS, BEATEN

1½ CUPS ALMOND FLOUR

½ TEASPOON KOSHER SALT

2 TABLESPOONS HEAVY CREAM

FOR THE TOP LAYER

⅓ CUP STEVIA OR PREFERRED KETO-FRIENDLY SWEETENER

8 OZ. CREAM CHEESE, AT ROOM TEMPERATURE

⅓ CUP HEAVY CREAM

2 TEASPOONS PURE VANILLA EXTRACT

PINCH OF KOSHER SALT

DIRECTIONS

1. Preheat the oven to 350°F and line a 9 x 13-inch baking pan with parchment paper. To prepare the base, place the butter, sweetener, and cocoa powder in a mixing bowl and stir until the mixture is thoroughly combined and smooth. Incorporate the eggs one at a time and then stir in the remaining ingredients. Work the mixture until it is a smooth batter and transfer it to the pan.

2. To prepare the top layer, place the sweetener in a food processor and pulse until it is fine and powdery. Add the remaining ingredients and blitz until combined. Spoon dollops of the mixture over the base and then spread them into an even layer.

3. Place the cake in the oven and bake for about 30 minutes, until it starts to pull away from the edges of the pan. Remove and let cool on a wire rack before slicing and serving.

Poppy Seed Swiss Roll

YIELD: **12 SERVINGS**
PREP TIME: **5 MINUTES**
COOKING TIME: **45 MINUTES**

NUTRITIONAL INFO:
(PER SERVING)
CALORIES: **285**
NET CARBS: **7.9 G**
CARBS: **13.2 G**
FAT: **24.8 G**
PROTEIN: **7.8 G**
FIBER: **5.3 G**

INGREDIENTS

FOR THE CAKE

⅔ CUP STEVIA OR PREFERRED KETO-FRIENDLY SWEETENER

6 LARGE EGGS

PINCH OF KOSHER SALT

1½ CUPS ALMOND FLOUR

3 TABLESPOONS POPPY SEEDS

2 TABLESPOONS PSYLLIUM HUSK POWDER

1 TEASPOON PURE VANILLA EXTRACT

FOR THE FILLING

¼ CUP STEVIA OR PREFERRED KETO-FRIENDLY SWEETENER, PLUS MORE TO TASTE

1⅔ CUPS HEAVY CREAM

3 OZ. RASPBERRIES, PLUS MORE FOR GARNISH

1¾ OZ. BLUEBERRIES

2½ OZ. SUGAR-FREE BITTERSWEET CHOCOLATE, CHOPPED, FOR GARNISH

DIRECTIONS

1. Preheat the oven to 375°F and line a rimmed 15 x 10–inch baking sheet with parchment paper. To begin preparations for the cake, place the sweetener, eggs, and salt in a large mixing bowl and beat until thick and frothy, about 5 minutes. Fold in the remaining ingredients, work the mixture until it is a smooth batter, and then pour the batter into the pan.

2. Place the cake in the oven and bake for about 15 minutes, until it is dry and springy to the touch. Remove and let cool on a wire rack for 5 minutes. Turn the cake out onto a sheet of parchment paper that is larger than the cake. Carefully roll the cake up into a cylinder and then wrap it in a kitchen towel.

3. To begin preparations for the filling, place the sweetener in a food processor and pulse until fine and powdery. Place it in a mixing bowl, add the cream, and beat until the mixture holds soft peaks.

4. Unroll the cake and spread about two-thirds of the whipped cream over it, leaving 1 inch of the perimeter of the cake uncovered. Dot with the raspberries and blueberries and then carefully roll it back up. Place on a platter and spread the remaining whipped cream over it.

5. Place the chocolate in a microwave-safe bowl and microwave on medium until melted, removing to stir every 15 seconds. Drizzle the chocolate over the cake, top with additional raspberries, and serve.

Chocolate & Cherry Cupcakes

YIELD: **8 SERVINGS**
PREP TIME: **10 MINUTES**
COOKING TIME: **35 MINUTES**

NUTRITIONAL INFO:
(PER SERVING)
CALORIES: **473**
NET CARBS: **8.2 G**
CARBS: **15.2 G**
FAT: **43.5 G**
PROTEIN: **9.4 G**
FIBER: **7 G**

INGREDIENTS

1 CUP ALMOND FLOUR

¼ CUP GOLDEN FLAXSEED MEAL

1½ TABLESPOONS COCONUT FLOUR

2 TEASPOONS BAKING POWDER

½ TEASPOON XANTHAN GUM

½ TEASPOON KOSHER SALT

1 STICK OF UNSALTED BUTTER, AT ROOM TEMPERATURE

¼ CUP HEAVY CREAM

¾ CUP UNSWEETENED COCOA POWDER

⅔ CUP STEVIA OR PREFERRED KETO-FRIENDLY SWEETENER

4 LARGE EGGS, AT ROOM TEMPERATURE

1 CUP CHOCOLATE FROSTING (SEE SIDEBAR)

8 CHERRIES, WITH STEMS

DIRECTIONS

1. Preheat the oven to 350°F and line a cupcake pan with eight paper wrappers. Place the almond flour, flaxseed meal, coconut flour, baking powder, xanthan gum, and salt in a mixing bowl and stir to combine. Place the butter, cream, and cocoa powder in a heatproof mixing bowl, place it over a half-full saucepan of simmering water, and whisk until the mixture is smooth. Remove from heat and let it cool for 5 minutes.

2. Stir the sweetener into the butter mixture and then incorporate the eggs one at a time. Gradually add the dry mixture and stir until the mixture is a smooth batter. Divide the batter between the wrappers, place in the oven, and bake, rotating the pan halfway through, for about 20 minutes, until a toothpick inserted into the centers of the cupcakes comes out clean. Remove and let cool on a wire rack.

3. Spread the frosting over the cupcakes, top each one with a cherry, and serve.

CHOCOLATE FROSTING

Place 2 sticks of unsalted butter in a large mixing bowl and beat with a handheld mixer until light and fluffy. Gradually add the ⅔ cup unsweetened cocoa powder, ⅓ cup stevia or preferred sweetener, ½ teaspoon pure vanilla extract, and 1 tablespoon heavy cream and beat until the mixture is smooth and fluffy, scraping down the sides of the bowl as needed. Use immediately or store the frosting in the refrigerator, where it will keep for up to 1 week. This preparation will produce 12 servings of frosting. The macros for each serving are as follows: 138 calories, 1.2 grams net carbs, 2 grams carbs, 14.5 grams fat, 0.5 grams protein, and 0.8 grams fiber.

Lemon & Poppy Seed Cupcakes

YIELD: **8 SERVINGS**
PREP TIME: **5 MINUTES**
COOKING TIME: **25 MINUTES**

NUTRITIONAL INFO:
(PER SERVING)
CALORIES: **226**
NET CARBS: **3 G**
CARBS: **5 G**
FAT: **21 G**
PROTEIN: **7 G**
FIBER: **2 G**

INGREDIENTS

4.9 OZ. ALMOND FLOUR

1½ TABLESPOONS POPPY SEEDS

½ TEASPOON BAKING POWDER

SALT, TO TASTE

JUICE AND ZEST OF 1 LEMON

6 TABLESPOONS UNSALTED BUTTER

3½ OZ. SUKRIN GOLD OR
PREFERRED KETO-FRIENDLY
SWEETENER

6 TABLESPOONS SOUR CREAM

½ TEASPOON PURE VANILLA
EXTRACT

2 EGGS

DIRECTIONS

1. Preheat the oven to 345°F and line a cupcake pan with eight paper wrappers. Place the almond flour, poppy seeds, baking powder, salt, and lemon zest in a mixing bowl and stir to combine.

2. Place the butter and sweetener in a mixing bowl and beat with a handheld mixer until pale and fluffy. If using a granulated sweetener, pulse 3 or 4 times in the blender before adding it to the butter so that it has an easier time dissolving.

3. Add the sour cream to the butter mixture and whisk to incorporate. Whisk in the vanilla, eggs, and lemon juice and then add the dry mixture. Stir until a smooth batter forms. Divide the batter between the wrappers, filling each two-thirds of the way.

4. Place in the oven and bake for about 25 minutes, until the cupcakes are golden brown and a toothpick inserted into the center of each one comes out clean. Remove from the oven and let cool before serving.

CHAPTER 2

COOKIES, BROWNIES & BARS

The recipes in this chapter are tailor-made for the busy individual, as they are preparations one can spend part of a Sunday afternoon making, and then have a sweet treat to nibble on for the rest of the week. Beyond classics like chocolate chip cookies and dark chocolate brownies, there are a few impressive options like the Chocolate & Hazelnut Kisses on page 101 that will wow anyone that comes past—no matter what diet they happen to be following.

Chocolate Chip Cookies

YIELD: **20 COOKIES**
PREP TIME: **5 MINUTES**
COOKING TIME: **35 MINUTES**

NUTRITIONAL INFO:
(PER SERVING)
CALORIES: **178**
NET CARBS: **5.1 G**
CARBS: **7.1 G**
FAT: **16.5 G**
PROTEIN: **2.5 G**
FIBER: **2 G**

INGREDIENTS

2 STICKS OF UNSALTED BUTTER

1½ CUPS ALMOND FLOUR

½ CUP COCONUT FLOUR

1½ TEASPOONS BAKING SODA

2 TABLESPOONS COCONUT OIL, MELTED

½ CUP STEVIA OR PREFERRED KETO-FRIENDLY SWEETENER

2 TEASPOONS PURE VANILLA EXTRACT

8 OZ. SUGAR-FREE SEMISWEET CHOCOLATE CHIPS

DIRECTIONS

1. Preheat the oven to 350°F and line two baking sheets with parchment paper.

2. Place the butter in a saucepan and cook over medium-high heat until it is dark brown and has a nutty aroma. Transfer to a heatproof mixing bowl.

3. Place the flours and baking soda in a bowl and whisk until combined.

4. Add the coconut oil, sweetener, and vanilla to the bowl containing the melted butter and whisk until combined. Gradually add the dry mixture and stir until incorporated. Add the chocolate chips and stir until evenly distributed. Form tablespoons of the mixture into balls and place them on the parchment-lined baking sheets, leaving about 2 inches between each ball. Gently press down on the balls to flatten them slightly.

5. Place the sheets in the oven and bake, while rotating the sheet halfway through, for about 12 minutes, until golden brown. Remove from the oven and let them cool on the baking sheets for 10 minutes before transferring to wire racks to cool completely.

Chocolate & Pistachio Cookies

YIELD: **12 COOKIES**
PREP TIME: **5 MINUTES**
COOKING TIME: **35 MINUTES**

NUTRITIONAL INFO:
(PER SERVING)
CALORIES: **148**
NET CARBS: **8.8 G**
CARBS: **15.3 G**
FAT: **12.9 G**
PROTEIN: **3.9 G**
FIBER: **6.5 G**

INGREDIENTS:

6¼ OZ. SUGAR-FREE SEMISWEET CHOCOLATE CHIPS

2 TABLESPOONS COCONUT OIL

⅓ CUP STEVIA OR PREFERRED KETO-FRIENDLY SWEETENER, PLUS MORE TO TASTE

1 LARGE EGG

1 TEASPOON PURE VANILLA EXTRACT

¼ TEASPOON BAKING POWDER

¼ TEASPOON KOSHER SALT

¼ CUP ALMOND FLOUR

1 TABLESPOON UNSWEETENED COCOA POWDER

1 OZ. SUGAR-FREE BITTERSWEET CHOCOLATE CHIPS

1¾ OZ. PISTACHIOS, CHOPPED

DIRECTIONS

1. Preheat the oven to 350°F and line two large baking sheets with parchment paper. Place the semisweet chocolate chips and coconut oil in a microwave-safe bowl and microwave on medium until melted, removing to stir every 10 seconds.

2. Place the sweetener, egg, vanilla, salt, and baking powder in a mixing bowl and stir until combined. Gradually stir in the melted chocolate mixture and then incorporate the almond flour and cocoa powder. Let the dough stand for 10 minutes.

3. Form tablespoons of the dough into balls, place them on the baking sheets, and gently press down on the balls to flatten them. Sprinkle the bittersweet chocolate chips and pistachios over each cookie.

4. Place the cookies in the oven and bake for about 12 minutes, until the edges are set. Remove from the oven and let them cool on the baking sheets before serving.

Peanut Butter & Chocolate Chip Cookies

YIELD: **20 COOKIES**
PREP TIME: **5 MINUTES**
COOKING TIME: **35 MINUTES**

NUTRITIONAL INFO:
(PER SERVING)
CALORIES: **191**
NET CARBS: **6.9 G**
CARBS: **9.3 G**
FAT: **16.1 G**
PROTEIN: **5.5 G**
FIBER: **2.4 G**

INGREDIENTS

8.8 OZ. SALTED, NO SUGAR ADDED PEANUT BUTTER

2 TABLESPOONS COCONUT OIL, MELTED

½ CUP STEVIA OR PREFERRED KETO-FRIENDLY SWEETENER

2 CUPS ALMOND FLOUR

1½ TEASPOONS BAKING SODA

2 TEASPOONS PURE VANILLA EXTRACT

5 OZ. SUGAR-FREE SEMISWEET CHOCOLATE CHIPS

DIRECTIONS

1. Preheat the oven to 350°F and line two baking sheets with parchment paper. Place all of the ingredients, except for the chocolate chips, in a mixing bowl and stir to combine. Add the chocolate chips and stir until evenly distributed.

2. Drop tablespoons of the dough on the baking sheets and gently press down to flatten them. Place in the oven and bake for about 12 minutes, until the edges are set and golden brown. Remove the cookies from the oven and let them cool on the baking sheets for 10 minutes before transferring to wire racks to cool completely.

Peanut Butter Cookies

YIELD: **10 COOKIES**
PREP TIME: **5 MINUTES**
COOKING TIME: **30 MINUTES**

NUTRITIONAL INFO:
(PER SERVING)
CALORIES: **115**
NET CARBS: **2.6 G**
CARBS: **4 G**
FAT: **9.6 G**
PROTEIN: **5.5 G**
FIBER: **1.4 G**

INGREDIENTS

4.4 OZ. SALTED, NO SUGAR ADDED PEANUT BUTTER

1 TABLESPOON COCONUT OIL, MELTED

⅓ CUP STEVIA OR PREFERRED KETO-FRIENDLY SWEETENER

1 CUP ALMOND FLOUR

¾ TEASPOON BAKING SODA

1 TEASPOON PURE VANILLA EXTRACT

½ TEASPOON FLAKY SEA SALT

DIRECTIONS

1. Preheat the oven to 350°F and line a large baking sheet with parchment paper. Place all of the ingredients, except for the salt, in a mixing bowl and stir to combine.

2. Drop tablespoons of the dough on the baking sheet, gently press down to flatten them, and then press down on them with a fork to leave a crosshatch pattern on top.

3. Place the cookies in the oven and bake for about 10 minutes, until the edges are set and golden brown. Remove from the oven and let the cookies cool on the baking sheet for 10 minutes before transferring to a wire rack to cool completely. Sprinkle the sea salt over the cookies before serving.

Chocolate & Almond Crinkle Cookies

YIELD: **24 COOKIES**
PREP TIME: **5 MINUTES**
COOKING TIME: **45 MINUTES**

NUTRITIONAL INFO:
(PER SERVING)
CALORIES: **106**
NET CARBS: **8 G**
CARBS: **9.6 G**
FAT: **8.8 G**
PROTEIN: **1.9 G**
FIBER: **1.6 G**

INGREDIENTS

2¼ OZ. SLIVERED ALMONDS

1 CUP STEVIA OR PREFERRED KETO-FRIENDLY SWEETENER

5 OZ. SUGAR-FREE CHOCOLATE CHIPS

¼ CUP HEAVY CREAM

1 STICK OF UNSALTED BUTTER, AT ROOM TEMPERATURE

2 LARGE EGGS, AT ROOM TEMPERATURE

½ TEASPOON PURE ALMOND EXTRACT

2 TABLESPOONS UNSWEETENED COCOA POWDER

2 TEASPOONS BAKING POWDER

½ TEASPOON KOSHER SALT

2 CUPS ALMOND FLOUR

¾ CUP COCONUT FLOUR

½ CUP SWERVE CONFECTIONERS'

DIRECTIONS

1. Preheat the oven to 350°F. Place the almonds on a baking sheet and toast for 5 to 7 minutes, until lightly browned. Remove from the oven and transfer to a food processor. Add 2 tablespoons of the sweetener and pulse until the mixture is very fine.

2. Place the chocolate and cream in a microwave-safe bowl and microwave on medium until melted and smooth, removing to stir in every 10 seconds.

3. Combine the butter and remaining sweetener in a mixing bowl and beat with a handheld mixer until light and fluffy. Incorporate the eggs one at a time and then fold in the chocolate mixture, cocoa powder, baking powder, and salt. Gradually add the flours and beat until a stiff dough forms. Stir in the almonds and place the dough in the refrigerator for 2 hours.

4. Preheat the oven to 350°F and line two baking sheets with parchment paper. Sift the confectioners' sweetener onto a sheet of waxed paper. Remove tablespoon-sized portions of the dough, form them into balls, and roll each ball in the confectioners' sweetener until evenly coated.

5. Place the balls 2 inches apart on the baking sheets, gently press down to flatten them slightly, place in oven, and bake for 14 to 16 minutes, until the cookies are cracking and the edges feel dry. Remove, let cool on the baking sheets for 5 minutes, and then transfer to wire racks to cool completely.

Almond Biscuits

YIELD: **24 BISCUITS**
(1 SERVING = 2 BISCUITS)
PREP TIME: **5 MINUTES**
COOKING TIME: **40 MINUTES**

NUTRITIONAL INFO:
(PER SERVING)
CALORIES: **157**
NET CARBS: **4.1 G**
CARBS: **7 G**
FAT: **12.9 G**
PROTEIN: **6.4 G**
FIBER: **2.9 G**

INGREDIENTS

¾ CUP STEVIA OR PREFERRED KETO-FRIENDLY SWEETENER

3 LARGE EGG WHITES

PINCH OF KOSHER SALT

2¾ CUPS ALMOND FLOUR

1½ TEASPOONS PURE ALMOND EXTRACT

1 TEASPOON CINNAMON

DIRECTIONS

1. Preheat the oven to 350°F and line two baking sheets with parchment paper. Place the sweetener in a food processor and pulse until fine and powdery. Place it in a bowl, add the egg whites and salt and beat until the mixture holds soft peaks. Add the almond flour and extract and fold until the mixture is a soft, smooth dough. Form generous teaspoons of the mixture into balls and place them on the baking sheets.

2. Gently press down on the balls to flatten them and sprinkle some cinnamon over each cookie. Place in the oven and bake for about 25 minutes, until the cookies are firm. Remove and let cool completely before serving.

Almond Clouds

YIELD: **24 COOKIES**
(1 SERVING = 1 COOKIE)
PREP TIME: **10 MINUTES**
COOKING TIME: **15 MINUTES**

NUTRITIONAL INFO:
(PER SERVING)
CALORIES: **117**
NET CARBS: **4.5 G**
CARBS: **6.1 G**
FAT: **10.6 G**
PROTEIN: **3.7 G**
FIBER: **1.6 G**

INGREDIENTS

4 TABLESPOONS UNSALTED
BUTTER, AT ROOM TEMPERATURE

2 OZ. CREAM CHEESE, AT ROOM
TEMPERATURE

⅓ CUP MONK FRUIT SWEETENER

1 LARGE EGG

1 TABLESPOON SOUR CREAM

1½ TEASPOONS PURE ALMOND
EXTRACT

½ TEASPOON PURE VANILLA
EXTRACT

PINCH OF KOSHER SALT

3 CUPS ALMOND FLOUR

24 ALMONDS

DIRECTIONS

1. Preheat the oven to 350°F and line a baking sheet with parchment paper. Place the butter, cream cheese, and sweetener in the bowl of a stand mixer and beat at medium speed until light and fluffy. Add the egg, sour cream, extracts, and salt and beat until thoroughly combined.

2. Reduce the mixer's speed to low and incorporate the almond flour ½ cup at a time. Form 1½-tablespoon portions of the dough into balls, place them on the baking sheet, and press down gently to flatten them. Press an almond into the center of each cookie.

3. Place the cookies in the oven and bake for about 15 minutes, until the edges are set and lightly browned. Remove and let the cookies cool on the baking sheet before serving.

Amaretti Cookies

YIELD: **4 SERVINGS**
PREP TIME: **15 MINUTES**
COOKING TIME: **30 MINUTES**

NUTRITIONAL INFO:
(PER SERVING)
CALORIES: **291**
NET CARBS: **4.8 G**
CARBS: **10.7 G**
FAT: **23.6 G**
PROTEIN: **13.7 G**
FIBER: **5.9 G**

INGREDIENTS

8 OZ. SLICED ALMONDS

½ CUP GRANULATED ERYTHRITOL

¼ CUP POWDERED ERYTHRITOL

4 LARGE EGG WHITES, AT ROOM
TEMPERATURE

½ TEASPOON CREAM OF TARTAR

PINCH OF KOSHER SALT

½ TEASPOON PURE ALMOND
EXTRACT

DIRECTIONS

1. Preheat the oven to 300°F and line two baking sheets with parchment paper. Place the almonds, granulated erythritol, and powdered erythritol in a food processor fitted and blitz until the mixture is finely ground.

2. Place the egg whites in a mixing bowl and beat with a handheld mixer until frothy. Add the cream of tartar, salt, and almond extract and beat until stiff peaks form. Fold the almond mixture into the meringue until no white streaks remain. Drop heaping tablespoons of the mixture onto the prepared baking sheets.

3. Place in the oven and bake for 15 minutes. Reverse their positions in the oven and bake for another 12 to 15 minutes, until the edges of the cookies begin to brown. Remove from the oven and let them cool completely on the baking sheets.

Almond & Orange Cookies

YIELD: **20 COOKIES**
PREP TIME: **5 MINUTES**
COOKING TIME: **1 HOUR AND 15 MINUTES**

NUTRITIONAL INFO:
(PER SERVING)
CALORIES: **148**
NET CARBS: **2.6 G**
CARBS: **4.3 G**
FAT: **13.6 G**
PROTEIN: **4 G**
FIBER: **1.7 G**

INGREDIENTS

1 CUP STEVIA OR PREFERRED KETO-FRIENDLY SWEETENER

3 CUPS ALMOND FLOUR, PLUS 3 TABLESPOONS AND MORE AS NEEDED

½ TEASPOON KOSHER SALT

10 TABLESPOONS UNSALTED BUTTER, AT ROOM TEMPERATURE

2 OZ. CREAM CHEESE, AT ROOM TEMPERATURE

2 TEASPOONS ORANGE ZEST

1 TEASPOON ORANGE BLOSSOM WATER

20 BLANCHED ALMONDS

DIRECTIONS

1. Place the sweetener in a food processor and pulse until fine and powdery. Add the almond flour and pulse until the mixture is just combined. Transfer the mixture to a mixing bowl, stir in the salt, and then incorporate the butter a tablespoon at a time, using a handheld mixer to beat the mixture until it is a moist crumble.

2. Stir in the cream cheese, orange zest, and orange blossom water. Turn out the dough and gently knead it until it holds together. Form the dough into a disk, envelop it in plastic wrap, and refrigerate for 1 hour.

3. Preheat the oven to 350°F and line two baking sheets with parchment paper. Remove the dough from the refrigerator and let it stand at room temperature for 5 to 10 minutes. Place it on a flour-dusted work surface and roll out to ¼ inch thick. Cut the dough into the desired shapes, place them on the baking sheets, and press an almond into each cookie. Place in the freezer for 15 minutes.

4. Place the cookies in the oven and bake for about 14 minutes, until the edges are set and golden brown. Remove from the oven and let the cookies cool on the baking sheets for 15 minutes before transferring them to wire racks to cool completely.

Lemon & Macadamia Cookies

YIELD: **24 COOKIES**
(1 SERVING = 3 COOKIES)
PREP TIME: **10 MINUTES**
COOKING TIME: **1 HOUR AND 15 MINUTES**

NUTRITIONAL INFO:
(PER SERVING)
CALORIES: **243**
NET CARBS: **5.7 G**
CARBS: **8.1 G**
FAT: **22.5 G**
PROTEIN: **4.5 G**
FIBER: **2.4 G**

INGREDIENTS

1¼ CUPS STEVIA OR PREFERRED KETO-FRIENDLY SWEETENER

3 TABLESPOONS MACADAMIA NUTS

1⅓ CUPS ALMOND FLOUR, PLUS MORE AS NEEDED

¼ TEASPOON KOSHER SALT

5 TABLESPOONS UNSALTED BUTTER, AT ROOM TEMPERATURE

2 TABLESPOONS CREAM CHEESE, AT ROOM TEMPERATURE

1 TEASPOON PURE LEMON EXTRACT

½ TEASPOON PURE VANILLA EXTRACT

1 TABLESPOON HEAVY CREAM

ZEST AND JUICE OF 1 LEMON

DIRECTIONS

1. Place ½ cup of the sweetener in a food processor and pulse until fine and powdery. Add the macadamia nuts and almond flour and pulse until the nuts are finely ground. Place the mixture in a mixing bowl and stir in the salt. Incorporate the butter 1 tablespoon at a time and work the mixture until it is a slightly moist crumble.

2. Stir in the cream cheese and extracts and knead the dough until it holds together. Form the dough into a disk, envelop it in plastic wrap, and refrigerate for 1 hour.

3. Preheat the oven to 350°F and line two baking sheets with parchment paper. Remove the dough from the fridge and let it stand at room temperature for 5 minutes. Place it on a flour-dusted work surface and roll out to ¼ inch thick. Cut the dough into the desired shapes and place them on the baking sheets. Store in the freezer for 15 minutes.

4. Place in the oven and bake for about 14 minutes, until the edges are set and golden brown. Remove and let cool on the baking sheets for 15 minutes before transferring to a wire rack to cool completely.

5. Place the remaining sweetener in a clean food processor and pulse until fine and powdery. Place it in a mixing bowl, add the cream and lemon juice, and stir until the mixture is smooth.

6. Spread the icing on the cookies and sprinkle the lemon zest on top. Let the icing set before serving.

Lemon & Coconut Snowballs

YIELD: **24 COOKIES**
(1 SERVING = 3 COOKIES)
PREP TIME: **5 MINUTES**
REFRIGERATION TIME: **30 MINUTES**

NUTRITIONAL INFO:
(PER SERVING)
CALORIES: **237**
NET CARBS: **1.7 G**
CARBS: **5.7 G**
FAT: **22.5 G**
PROTEIN: **5.1 G**
FIBER: **4 G**

INGREDIENTS

1 CUP ALMOND FLOUR

3 OZ. UNSWEETENED SHREDDED COCONUT

⅓ CUP STEVIA OR PREFERRED KETO-FRIENDLY SWEETENER

ZEST AND JUICE OF ½ LEMON

4 OZ. CREAM CHEESE, AT ROOM TEMPERATURE

1 TEASPOON PURE VANILLA EXTRACT

DIRECTIONS

1. Place the almond flour, two-thirds of the coconut, and the sweetener in a large mixing bowl and stir to combine. Place the remaining coconut in a shallow bowl and set aside.

2. Add the remaining ingredients and stir until the mixture is a rough dough. Form tablespoons of the dough into balls and then roll them in the coconut. Place the cookies on a tray, cover with plastic wrap, and refrigerate for 30 minutes before serving.

Cashew Macaroons

YIELD: **12 SERVINGS**
(1 SERVING = 3 COOKIES)
PREP TIME: **10 MINUTES**
COOKING TIME: **10 MINUTES**

NUTRITIONAL INFO:
(PER SERVING)
CALORIES: **161**
NET CARBS: **8.1 G**
CARBS: **9 G**
FAT: **12.8 G**
PROTEIN: **4.8 G**
FIBER: **0.9 G**

INGREDIENTS

10.6 OZ. RAW CASHEWS,
PLUS 36 FOR GARNISH

1¼ CUPS GRANULATED
ERYTHRITOL

2 LARGE EGG WHITES

PINCH OF KOSHER SALT

½ TEASPOON PURE VANILLA
EXTRACT

DIRECTIONS

1. Preheat the oven to 350°F and line two baking sheets with parchment paper. Place the cashews and erythritol in a food processor and blitz until the nuts are finely ground. Add the egg whites, salt, and vanilla and pulse until combined.

2. Form tablespoons of the dough into balls, place them on the baking sheets, and press a cashew into each ball. Place in the oven and bake for 10 to 12 minutes, or until lightly brown. Remove and let the cookies cool for 5 minutes on the baking sheets before transferring to wire racks to cool completely.

Coconut Macaroons

YIELD: **12 SERVINGS**
(1 SERVING = 3 COOKIES)
PREP TIME: **15 MINUTES**
COOKING TIME: **30 MINUTES**

NUTRITIONAL INFO:
(PER SERVING)
CALORIES: **96**
NET CARBS: **2.1 G**
CARBS: **3.9 G**
FAT: **9 G**
PROTEIN: **2.4 G**
FIBER: **1.8 G**

INGREDIENTS

8.4 OZ. UNSWEETENED SHREDDED COCONUT

5 LARGE EGG WHITES, AT ROOM TEMPERATURE

½ TEASPOON CREAM OF TARTAR

¼ TEASPOON KOSHER SALT

½ CUP GRANULATED ERYTHRITOL

½ CUP POWDERED ERYTHRITOL

1 TEASPOON PURE VANILLA EXTRACT

DIRECTIONS

1. Preheat the oven to 350°F and line two baking sheets with parchment paper. Place the coconut on another baking sheet, place it in the oven, and toast for 7 to 10 minutes, until lightly browned. Remove and let the coconut cool. Reduce the oven temperature to 275°F.

2. Place the egg whites in a mixing bowl and beat with a handheld mixer until frothy. Add the cream of tartar and salt and beat until soft peaks form. Incorporate both forms of erythritol a tablespoon at a time and beat until the mixture holds stiff peaks. Stir in the vanilla and then fold the toasted coconut into the meringue.

3. Drop heaping tablespoons of the mixture onto the baking sheets, leaving about 1½ inches between them. Place in the oven and bake for 25 to 30 minutes, until the macaroons are dry to the touch. Remove and place the baking sheets on wire racks to cool.

White Chocolate & Pistachio Meringues

YIELD: **6 SERVINGS**
PREP TIME: **5 MINUTES**
COOKING TIME: **1 HOUR AND 20 MINUTES**

NUTRITIONAL INFO:
(PER SERVING)
CALORIES: **70**
NET CARBS: **5.4 G**
CARBS: **6.4 G**
FAT: **4.3 G**
PROTEIN: **2.1 G**
FIBER: **1 G**

INGREDIENTS

2 LARGE EGG WHITES, AT ROOM TEMPERATURE

PINCH OF KOSHER SALT

½ TEASPOON CREAM OF TARTAR

4 TEASPOONS STEVIA OR PREFERRED KETO-FRIENDLY SWEETENER

¼ TEASPOON PURE VANILLA EXTRACT

1¼ OZ. SUGAR-FREE WHITE CHOCOLATE CHIPS

2 TABLESPOONS CHOPPED PISTACHIOS

DIRECTIONS

1. Preheat the oven to 200°F and line a large rimmed baking sheet with parchment paper. Place the egg whites, salt, and cream of tartar in a mixing bowl and beat until the mixture holds medium peaks.

2. Melt the sweetener in a small saucepan over a low heat, swirling occasionally. Remove from heat, add the vanilla, and swirl the pan to combine. Gradually incorporate the mixture into the whipped cream, taking care not to overwork the mixture.

3. Spoon mounds of the meringue onto the baking sheet, leaving plenty of space between. Place in the oven and bake until set and dry to the touch, about 45 minutes. Turn off the oven and let the meringues cool completely in the oven.

4. Place the white chocolate chips in a microwave-safe bowl and microwave on medium until melted, removing to stir every 10 seconds. Drizzle over the meringues and then sprinkle the pistachios over the top. Let the chocolate set before serving.

Chocolate & Hazelnut Kisses

YIELD: **6 SERVINGS**
PREP TIME: **5 MINUTES**
COOKING TIME: **1 HOUR AND 25 MINUTES**

NUTRITIONAL INFO:
(PER SERVING)
CALORIES: **228**
NET CARBS: **8.9 G**
CARBS: **10.2 G**
FAT: **20.6 G**
PROTEIN: **3.7 G**
FIBER: **1.3 G**

INGREDIENTS

3 LARGE EGG WHITES, AT ROOM TEMPERATURE

PINCH OF KOSHER SALT

¾ TEASPOON CREAM OF TARTAR

4 TEASPOONS STEVIA OR PREFERRED KETO-FRIENDLY SWEETENER

½ TEASPOON PURE VANILLA EXTRACT

3⅓ OZ. SUGAR-FREE BITTERSWEET CHOCOLATE CHIPS

⅔ CUP HEAVY CREAM

2 TABLESPOONS FINELY GROUND HAZELNUTS

2 TABLESPOONS UNSALTED BUTTER

DIRECTIONS

1. Preheat the oven to 200°F and line a large rimmed baking sheet with parchment paper. Place the egg whites, salt, and cream of tartar in a mixing bowl and beat until the mixture holds medium peaks.

2. Melt the sweetener in a small saucepan over a low heat, swirling occasionally. Remove from heat, add the vanilla, and swirl the pan to combine. Gradually incorporate the mixture into the whipped cream, taking care not to overwork the mixture. Spoon the meringue into a piping bag fitted with a round piping tip and pipe 12 large "kisses" onto the baking sheet, leaving plenty of space between them.

3. Place in the oven and bake until set and dry to the touch, about 50 minutes. Turn off the oven and let the meringues cool completely in the oven.

4. Place the chocolate chips in a heatproof bowl. Warm the cream in a small saucepan. When it starts to simmer, pour it over the chocolate and let stand for 2 minutes before adding the butter and hazelnuts. Stir until the mixture is smooth and thick. Cover the bowl with plastic wrap and refrigerate for 15 minutes.

5. Spread the hazelnut-and-chocolate mixture on the underside of one of the kisses and press the underside of another one against it to form sandwiches. Serve immediately.

Gingerbread Cookies

YIELD: **20 COOKIES**
PREP TIME: **15 MINUTES**
COOKING TIME: **15 MINUTES**

NUTRITIONAL INFORMATION:
(PER SERVING)
CALORIES: **140**
NET CARBS: **3 G**
CARBS: **4.9 G**
FAT: **12.6 G**
PROTEIN: **4 G**
FIBER: **1.9 G**

INGREDIENTS

1 CUP POWDERED ERYTHRITOL

⅔ CUP ALMOND MEAL

2½ CUPS ALMOND FLOUR, PLUS
MORE AS NEEDED

½ TEASPOON KOSHER SALT

2 TEASPOONS GROUND GINGER

1 TEASPOON CINNAMON

1 TEASPOON GRATED FRESH
NUTMEG

6 TABLESPOONS UNSALTED
BUTTER, AT ROOM TEMPERATURE

2 OZ. CREAM CHEESE, AT ROOM
TEMPERATURE

1 TEASPOON ORANGE ZEST

DIRECTIONS

1. Place the erythritol, almond meal, and almond flour in a food processor and pulse until combined.

2. Transfer the mixture to a mixing bowl and stir in the salt, ground ginger, cinnamon, and nutmeg. Incorporate the butter 1 tablespoon at a time and work the mixture with a pastry blender until it is a coarse crumble. Add the cream cheese and orange zest, stir to incorporate, and then knead the mixture until it is a smooth dough, incorporating more almond flour as needed. Envelop the dough in plastic wrap and refrigerate it for 1 hour.

3. Preheat the oven to 350°F and line two baking sheets with parchment paper. Remove the dough from the refrigerator and let it stand at room temperature for 5 to 10 minutes.

4. Place the dough on a flour-dusted work surface and roll it out to about ¼ inch thick. Cut the dough into the desired shapes and place them on the baking sheets. Freeze the cookies for 15 minutes.

5. Place the cookies in the oven and bake for about 15 minutes, until the edges are set and golden brown. Remove from the oven and let the cookies cool on the sheets for 15 minutes before transferring to a wire rack to cool completely. If desired, decorate the cookies with some of the Sugar Glaze on page 109.

Ginger Shortbread

YIELD: **12 SERVINGS**
PREP TIME: **5 MINUTES**
COOKING TIME: **40 MINUTES**

NUTRITIONAL INFO:
(PER SERVING)
CALORIES: **183**
NET CARBS: **2.8 G**
CARBS: **4.8 G**
FAT: **17.1 G**
PROTEIN: **4.5 G**
FIBER: **2 G**

INGREDIENTS

2 CUPS ALMOND FLOUR

⅓ CUP STEVIA OR PREFERRED
KETO-FRIENDLY SWEETENER

1-INCH PIECE OF FRESH GINGER,
PEELED AND MINCED

1 TEASPOON GROUND GINGER

¼ TEASPOON KOSHER SALT

1 TEASPOON PURE VANILLA
EXTRACT

1 STICK OF UNSALTED BUTTER,
AT ROOM TEMPERATURE

1 LARGE EGG, LIGHTLY BEATEN

DIRECTIONS

1. Preheat the oven to 300°F and line a square 8-inch baking pan with parchment paper. Place the almond flour, sweetener, fresh ginger, ground ginger, salt, and vanilla in a mixing bowl and stir to combine. Stir in the butter and the egg and work the mixture until it is a soft dough.

2. Press the dough into the pan, making sure the top is flat and even. Use a fork to segment the dough into neat rows. Place in the oven and bake for about 30 minutes, until set and golden brown. Remove and let cool completely on a wire rack before cutting into bars.

Orange & Rosemary Shortbread

YIELD: **12 SERVINGS**
PREP TIME: **15 MINUTES**
COOKING TIME: **30 MINUTES**

NUTRITIONAL INFORMATION:
(PER SERVING)
CALORIES: **395**
NET CARBS: **2.9 G**
CARBS: **4.9 G**
FAT: **17.1 G**
PROTEIN: **4.5 G**
FIBER: **2 G**

INGREDIENTS

2 CUPS ALMOND FLOUR, PLUS
MORE AS NEEDED

⅓ CUP GRANULATED ERYTHRITOL

1 TABLESPOON ORANGE ZEST

2 TEASPOONS FINELY CHOPPED
FRESH ROSEMARY

¼ TEASPOON KOSHER SALT

1 TEASPOON PURE VANILLA
EXTRACT

½ TEASPOON ORANGE BLOSSOM
WATER

1 STICK OF UNSALTED BUTTER,
AT ROOM TEMPERATURE

1 LARGE EGG, LIGHTLY BEATEN

DIRECTIONS

1. Preheat the oven to 300°F and line a baking sheet with parchment paper. Place the almond flour, erythritol, orange zest, rosemary, salt, vanilla, and orange blossom water in a mixing bowl and stir to combine.

2. Add the butter and work the mixture with a pastry blender until it is a coarse crumble. Incorporate the egg and work the mixture until it is a soft dough.

3. Place the dough on a flour-dusted work surface and roll it out to approximately ¼ inch thick. Cut 12 rounds out of the dough and place them on the baking sheet.

4. Place the cookies in the oven and bake for about 30 minutes, until the edges are set and the tops are golden brown. Remove from the oven and let the cookies cool on the pan before serving.

Sugar Glaze

YIELD: **24 SERVINGS (2 CUPS)**
PREP TIME: **5 MINUTES**
COOKING TIME: **5 MINUTES**

NUTRITIONAL INFO:
(PER SERVING)
CALORIES: **48**
NET CARBS: **4 G**
CARBS: **11.9 G**
FAT: **0 G**
PROTEIN: **0 G**
FIBER: **7.9 G**

INGREDIENTS

2 CUPS STEVIA OR PREFERRED
KETO-FRIENDLY SWEETENER

HOT WATER (125°F), AS NEEDED

1 TEASPOON PURE VANILLA
EXTRACT

DIRECTIONS

1. Place the sweetener in a food processor and pulse until fine and powdery.

2. Transfer to a mixing bowl and stir in teaspoons of hot water until the mixture is smooth and spreadable. Stir in the vanilla and use immediately or store in the refrigerator, where it will keep for up to 1 week. This glaze can be applied to any of the cakes or cookies in this book.

Dark Chocolate & Stout Brownies

YIELD: **16 SERVINGS**
PREP TIME: **5 MINUTES**
COOKING TIME: **1 HOUR AND 20 MINUTES**

NUTRITIONAL INFO
(PER SERVING)
CALORIES: **244**
NET CARBS: **11.8 G**
CARBS: **14.1 G**
FAT: **20.3 G**
PROTEIN: **2.6 G**
FIBER: **2.3 G**

INGREDIENTS

2 STICKS OF UNSALTED BUTTER, PLUS MORE AS NEEDED

1¼ CUPS GUINNESS

11 OZ. SUGAR-FREE DARK CHOCOLATE CHIPS

3 LARGE EGGS

1 TEASPOON PURE VANILLA EXTRACT

¾ CUP ALMOND FLOUR

1 TEASPOON KOSHER SALT

¼ CUP UNSWEETENED COCOA POWDER

DIRECTIONS

1. Preheat the oven to 350°F and grease an 8-inch square cake pan with butter. Place the stout in a medium saucepan, bring to a boil, and cook until it has reduced by half. Remove the pan from heat and let cool.

2. Place the chocolate chips and butter in a microwave-safe bowl and microwave on medium until melted, removing to stir every 15 seconds.

3. Place the eggs and vanilla in a large mixing bowl and whisk until combined. Slowly whisk in the chocolate-and-butter mixture and then whisk in the reduced stout. Fold in the almond flour and salt and then pour the batter into the pan.

4. Place in the oven and bake for about 35 minutes, until the surface begins to crack and a toothpick inserted into the center comes out with a few moist crumbs attached. Remove from the oven and let cool.

5. To serve, sprinkle the cocoa powder over the brownies and cut them into squares.

Marble Brownies

YIELD: **12 SERVINGS**
PREP TIME: **5 MINUTES**
COOKING TIME: **50 MINUTES**

NUTRITIONAL INFO:
(PER SERVING)
CALORIES: **230**
NET CARBS: **6.8 G**
CARBS: **8.1 G**
FAT: **20.8 G**
PROTEIN: **4.5 G**
FIBER: **1.3 G**

INGREDIENTS

1 STICK OF UNSALTED BUTTER, PLUS 1 TABLESPOON

¾ CUP ALMOND FLOUR, PLUS MORE AS NEEDED

5½ OZ. SUGAR-FREE SEMISWEET CHOCOLATE CHIPS

3 LARGE EGGS, AT ROOM TEMPERATURE

¾ CUP STEVIA OR PREFERRED KETO-FRIENDLY SWEETENER

PINCH OF KOSHER SALT

8 OZ. CREAM CHEESE, AT ROOM TEMPERATURE

½ TEASPOON PURE VANILLA EXTRACT

DIRECTIONS

1. Preheat the oven to 350°F. Grease an 8-inch square cake pan with the tablespoon of butter and sprinkle almond flour over it, making sure to tip out any excess.

2. Place the remaining butter and chocolate chips in a microwave-safe bowl and microwave on medium until melted, removing to stir every 15 seconds. Let cool for 5 minutes.

3. Place two of the eggs and ½ cup of the sweetener in a mixing bowl and beat with a handheld mixer for 1 minute. Add the chocolate mixture, beat until thoroughly incorporated, and then incorporate the almond flour and salt. Pour the mixture into the cake pan.

4. In a separate bowl, combine the cream cheese, remaining egg and sweetener, and the vanilla. Beat until light and fluffy and spread the mixture on top of the batter in the pan. Use a fork to swirl the two batters together.

5. Place in the oven and bake for about 30 minutes, until the top is springy to the touch. Remove from the oven and let the brownies cool completely before cutting them into squares.

Chocolate & Macadamia Brownies

YIELD: **16 SERVINGS**
PREP TIME: **5 MINUTES**
COOKING TIME: **40 MINUTES**

NUTRITIONAL INFO:
(PER SERVING)
CALORIES: **157**
NET CARBS: **5.8 G**
CARBS: **7.6 G**
FAT: **14.1 G**
PROTEIN: **3 G**
FIBER: **1.8 G**

INGREDIENTS

3⅓ OZ. SUGAR-FREE BITTERSWEET CHOCOLATE CHIPS

5 TABLESPOONS UNSALTED BUTTER

½ CUP STEVIA OR PREFERRED KETO-FRIENDLY SWEETENER

2 LARGE EGGS

2 TABLESPOONS COCONUT MILK OR COCONUT CREAM

1 TEASPOON PURE VANILLA EXTRACT

⅔ CUP ALMOND FLOUR

2 TABLESPOONS UNSWEETENED COCOA POWDER

½ TEASPOON BAKING POWDER

¼ TEASPOON KOSHER SALT

⅔ CUP CHOPPED MACADAMIA NUTS

DIRECTIONS

1. Preheat the oven to 350°F. Line an 8-inch square cake pan with parchment paper and spray it with nonstick cooking spray. Melt the chocolate chips and butter in a small saucepan over medium heat, stirring occasionally. Remove the pan from heat and set it aside.

2. Place the sweetener, eggs, coconut milk or coconut cream, and vanilla in a large mixing bowl and beat until the mixture is pale and thick. Place the almond flour, cocoa powder, baking powder, and salt in a separate mixing bowl and stir until thoroughly combined.

3. Gradually add the chocolate mixture to the egg mixture and stir until thoroughly incorporated. Working in three batches, fold in the almond flour mixture and then fold in the macadamia nuts. Pour the batter into the loaf pan.

4. Place in the oven and bake for about 20 minutes, until the brownies are dry to the touch and golden brown on top. A toothpick inserted into the center should come out with a few crumbs attached. Remove and let cool before slicing and serving.

No-Bake Hazelnut Brownies

YIELD: **16 SERVINGS**

PREP TIME: **5 MINUTES**

REFRIGERATION TIME: **1 HOUR**

NUTRITIONAL INFO:
(PER SERVING)

CALORIES: **186**

NET CARBS: **7.9 G**

CARBS: **10.3 G**

FAT: **16.7 G**

PROTEIN: **3 G**

FIBER: **2.4 G**

INGREDIENTS

FOR THE BROWNIES

5 TABLESPOONS UNSALTED BUTTER

5 OZ. SUGAR-FREE CHOCOLATE CHIPS

½ CUP ALMOND FLOUR

3 TABLESPOONS UNSWEETENED COCOA POWDER

½ CUP STEVIA OR PREFERRED KETO-FRIENDLY SWEETENER

FOR THE TOPPING

3 TABLESPOONS UNSWEETENED ALMOND MILK

3¾ OZ. SUGAR-FREE CHOCOLATE CHIPS

1½ TABLESPOONS STEVIA OR PREFERRED KETO-FRIENDLY SWEETENER

¼ TEASPOON KOSHER SALT

2 TABLESPOONS COCONUT OIL

5 OZ. HAZELNUTS, CHOPPED

DIRECTIONS

1. To begin preparations for the brownies, place the butter and ⅔ cup of the chocolate chips in a microwave-safe bowl and microwave on medium until melted, removing to stir every 15 seconds.

2. Add the remaining chocolate chips and stir until melted. Add the almond flour, cocoa powder, and sweetener and stir until the mixture is a smooth batter. Pour it into a square 8-inch cake pan, cover with plastic wrap, and refrigerate for 1 hour.

3. To prepare the topping, warm the almond milk in a small saucepan over medium heat until it starts to simmer. Pour it into a mixing bowl and add the chocolate chips, sweetener, salt, and coconut oil. Let the mixture stand for 2 minutes before gently stirring until it is smooth. Refrigerate for 10 minutes, spread over the brownies, and sprinkle the hazelnuts over the top.

Coconut Blondies

YIELD: **8 SERVINGS**
PREP TIME: **10 MINUTES**
COOKING TIME: **20 MINUTES**

NUTRITIONAL INFO:
(PER SERVING)
CALORIES: **161**
NET CARBS: **4 G**
CARBS: **6 G**
FAT: **13.4 G**
PROTEIN: **4.6 G**
FIBER: **2 G**

INGREDIENTS

⅓ CUP VEGETABLE OIL

3 LARGE EGGS

¼ CUP COCONUT CREAM

1 TEASPOON PURE VANILLA
EXTRACT

½ CUP COCONUT FLOUR

⅓ CUP POWDERED ERYTHRITOL

1 TEASPOON BAKING POWDER

PINCH OF KOSHER SALT

1.4 OZ. UNSWEETENED
SHREDDED COCONUT

DIRECTIONS

1. Preheat the oven to 350°F and line a square 8-inch cake
    pan with parchment paper. Place the oil, eggs, coconut
    cream, and vanilla in a food processor and puree until
    smooth. Add the coconut flour, erythritol, baking powder,
    salt, and half of the coconut and blitz until combined.

2. Transfer the mixture to the pan and sprinkle the
    remaining coconut over the top. Place in the oven and
    bake for about 20 minutes, until the edges are browned.
    Remove from the oven and let the pan cool on a wire
    rack before slicing.

Maple Walnut Bars

YIELD: **12 SERVINGS**
PREP TIME: **15 MINUTES**
COOKING TIME: **20 MINUTES**

NUTRITIONAL INFO:
(PER SERVING)
CALORIES: **285**
NET CARBS: **4.9 G**
CARBS: **7.6 G**
FAT: **26.6 G**
PROTEIN: **8.1 G**
FIBER: **2.7 G**

INGREDIENTS

4.4 OZ. WALNUTS, CHOPPED

2 CUPS ALMOND FLOUR

3 TABLESPOONS UNSALTED
BUTTER, MELTED AND COOLED
TO ROOM TEMPERATURE

¾ CUP GRANULATED ERYTHRITOL

1 LARGE EGG YOLK

1 LARGE EGG

8 OZ. CREAM CHEESE, AT ROOM
TEMPERATURE

2 TABLESPOONS SOUR CREAM

1 TEASPOON PURE MAPLE EXTRACT

PINCH OF KOSHER SALT

DIRECTIONS

1. Preheat the oven to 350°F and line a 9 x 13–inch baking pan with parchment paper. Place the walnuts on a baking sheet, place them in the oven, and toast for 5 to 7 minutes, or until lightly browned. Remove the nuts from the oven and set aside.

2. Place the almond flour, butter, ⅓ cup of the erythritol, and the egg yolk in a mixing bowl and stir to combine. Press the mixture into the baking sheet, place it in the oven, and bake for about 10 minutes, until it is set. Remove the pan from the oven.

3. Place the egg, cream cheese, sour cream, maple extract, salt, and remaining erythritol in a mixing bowl and beat with a handheld mixer until smooth. Spread the mixture over the crust and then sprinkle the toasted walnuts on top.

4. Place in the oven and bake for about 20 minutes, until the topping is set. Remove and let the bars cool to room temperature. Refrigerate for at least 4 hours before cutting and serving.

Lime Bars

YIELD: **8 SERVINGS**
PREP TIME: **15 MINUTES**
COOKING TIME: **45 MINUTES**

NUTRITIONAL INFO:
(PER SERVING)
CALORIES: **275**
NET CARBS: **3.9 G**
CARBS: **6.6 G**
FAT: **25.6 G**
PROTEIN: **7.8 G**
FIBER: **2.7 G**

INGREDIENTS

3 LIMES

1 STICK OF UNSALTED BUTTER,
MELTED AND COOLED TO ROOM
TEMPERATURE

1¾ CUPS ALMOND FLOUR

1 CUP POWDERED ERYTHRITOL

PINCH OF KOSHER SALT

3 LARGE EGGS

DIRECTIONS

1. Preheat the oven to 350°F and line a square 8-inch cake pan with parchment paper. Grate the zest of two of the limes into a mixing bowl. Squeeze the juice from all of the limes into the bowl and set it aside.

2. Place the butter, 1 cup of the almond flour, ¼ cup of the erythritol, and the salt in a mixing bowl and stir to combine. Press the mixture into the bottom of the prepared pan. Place it in the oven and bake for 20 minutes, until it starts to brown. Remove and allow to cool for 10 minutes.

3. Add the remaining almond flour and erythritol, and the eggs in the bowl with the lime juice and lime zest. Stir until thoroughly combined and then pour the mixture over the crust.

4. Place in the oven and bake for about 25 minutes, until the topping is set. Remove and let cool completely before cutting into bars.

Muesli Bars

YIELD: **8 SERVINGS**
PREP TIME: **5 MINUTES**
COOKING TIME: **40 MINUTES**

NUTRITIONAL INFO:
(PER SERVING)
CALORIES: **270**
NET CARBS: **9 G**
CARBS: **14 G**
FAT: **23 G**
PROTEIN: **6.1 G**
FIBER: **5 G**

INGREDIENTS:

2½ OZ. WHOLE ALMONDS

1¾ OZ. PECAN HALVES

4 OZ. SLICED ALMONDS

2 OZ. UNSWEETENED SHREDDED COCONUT

1 LARGE EGG

¼ CUP STEVIA OR PREFERRED KETO-FRIENDLY SWEETENER, PLUS MORE TO TASTE

2 TABLESPOONS NO SUGAR ADDED ALMOND BUTTER

1 TABLESPOON COCONUT OIL

¾ TEASPOON FLAKY SEA SALT

3⅓ OZ. SUGAR-FREE SEMISWEET CHOCOLATE CHIPS

DIRECTIONS

1. Preheat the oven to 375°F and line a square 8-inch cake pan with parchment paper. Place all of the nuts on a baking sheet. Place the coconut on a separate baking sheet. Place them in the oven and toast until golden brown, 3 to 4 minutes for the coconut, and 5 to 7 minutes for the nuts. Remove from the oven and let cool completely. Reduce the oven's temperature to 350°F.

2. Place the egg and sweetener in a large mixing bowl and stir to combine. Place the almond butter and coconut oil in a microwave-safe bowl and microwave until liquefied, removing to stir every 10 seconds. Stir this mixture into the mixing bowl and then fold in the nuts, coconut, salt, and chocolate chips. Work the mixture until thoroughly combined and then place it in the baking pan. Press it firmly into the pan, making sure the top is even.

3. Place in the oven and bake for about 15 minutes, until the top is just set. Remove and let cool completely before slicing into bars.

Chocolate & Coconut Bars

YIELD: **16 SERVINGS**
PREP TIME: **5 MINUTES**
COOKING TIME: **50 MINUTES**

NUTRITIONAL INFO:
(PER SERVING)
CALORIES: **316**
NET CARBS: **9.2 G**
CARBS: **12.4 G**
FAT: **29.2 G**
PROTEIN: **5.2 G**
FIBER: **3.2 G**

INGREDIENTS

1 STICK OF UNSALTED BUTTER, PLUS 1 TABLESPOON

½ CUP COCONUT OIL

1 CUP STEVIA OR PREFERRED KETO-FRIENDLY SWEETENER

3 LARGE EGGS, AT ROOM TEMPERATURE

1 TEASPOON PURE VANILLA EXTRACT

½ CUP UNSWEETENED COCOA POWDER

1 TEASPOON BAKING SODA

½ TEASPOON KOSHER SALT

1½ CUPS ALMOND FLOUR

½ CUP COCONUT FLOUR

5 OZ. SUGAR-FREE SEMISWEET CHOCOLATE CHIPS

8 OZ. CREAM CHEESE, AT ROOM TEMPERATURE

¼ CUP HEAVY CREAM

3 OZ. UNSWEETENED SHREDDED COCONUT

DIRECTIONS

1. Preheat the oven to 375°F and grease a 9 x 13-inch baking dish with the tablespoon of butter. Combine the remaining butter, coconut oil, and sweetener in a mixing bowl and beat with a handheld mixer until light and fluffy.

2. Add the eggs and vanilla and beat until well combined. Add the cocoa powder, baking soda, and salt and beat at medium speed. Reduce the speed to low, add the flours, beat until incorporated, and then fold in the chocolate chips.

3. Pour the batter in the pan and use a rubber spatula to spread it evenly. Place the cream cheese and cream in a small bowl and beat until combined. Stir in the coconut and then spread this mixture in an even layer on top of the batter. Place the pan in the oven and bake for 25 to 30 minutes, until a toothpick comes out clean after being inserted into the center. Remove from the oven, allow to cool in the pan, and then cut into bars.

CHAPTER 3

TARTS & PIES

The most enjoyable way of conveying your favorite confections is typically a tart or a pie. Simply fill a light, flaky crust with your desired treat, and you're off. With that in mind, we offer preparations for both a tart shell and several piecrusts, so that you have a way to contain whatever you whip up, or put a spin on what's provided within. There's also a few standbys that will provide some solace when you don't know where to turn on your own.

Tart Pastry Shell

YIELD: **1 TART SHELL (10 SERVINGS)**
PREP TIME: **5 MINUTES**
COOKING TIME: **50 MINUTES**

NUTRITIONAL INFO:
(PER SERVING)
CALORIES: **170**
NET CARBS: **3.1 G**
CARBS: **5.4 G**
FAT: **15.4 G**
PROTEIN: **3.6 G**
FIBER: **2.3 G**

INGREDIENTS

1 LARGE EGG YOLK

1 TABLESPOON HEAVY CREAM

½ TEASPOON PURE VANILLA
EXTRACT

1¼ CUPS ALMOND FLOUR, PLUS
MORE AS NEEDED

⅓ CUP COCONUT FLOUR

½ CUP STEVIA OR PREFERRED
KETO-FRIENDLY SWEETENER

¼ TEASPOON KOSHER SALT

1 STICK OF UNSALTED BUTTER,
CHILLED

DIRECTIONS

1. Whisk together the egg yolk, cream, and vanilla in a small mixing bowl. Set the mixture aside.

2. Place the flours, sweetener, and salt in a food processor and pulse until combined. Incorporate the butter 1 tablespoon at a time and pulse until the mixture is coarse crumbs. Set the speed to low and gradually incorporate the egg yolk mixture until a dough forms.

3. Place the dough on a sheet of plastic wrap and pat down to flatten it into a disc. Envelop in the plastic wrap and refrigerate for 2 hours.

4. Remove the dough from the refrigerator and let it rest at room temperature for 5 to 10 minutes. Preheat the oven to 350°F. Place the dough on a flour-dusted work surface and roll it out.

5. Place it in a tart pan, prick the dough with a fork, and line it with parchment paper. Fill with uncooked rice or dried beans, place it in the oven, and bake for about 20 minutes, until golden brown and dry to the touch at the edges. Remove from the oven, discard the parchment paper and uncooked rice or dried beans, and return the shell to the oven. Bake for another 8 minutes, remove from the oven, and let cool completely before filling.

Perfect Piecrust

YIELD: **1 PIECRUST (10 SERVINGS)**
PREP TIME: **5 MINUTES**
REFRIGERATION TIME: **1 HOUR**

NUTRITIONAL INFO:
(PER SERVING)
CALORIES: **153**
NET CARBS: **2.4 G**
CARBS: **4.5 G**
FAT: **14.2 G**
PROTEIN: **4.2 G**
FIBER: **2.1 G**

INGREDIENTS

1¾ CUPS ALMOND FLOUR

2 TABLESPOONS STEVIA OR
PREFERRED KETO-FRIENDLY
SWEETENER

½ TEASPOON KOSHER SALT

4 TABLESPOONS UNSALTED
BUTTER, MELTED

1 TABLESPOON ICE WATER

DIRECTIONS

1. Whisk together the almond flour, sweetener, and salt in a mixing bowl. Stir in the butter and ice water and work the mixture with a fork until it is coarse crumbs.

2. Transfer the mixture to a 9-inch pie plate and press it into the base and up the side. Prick the crust all over with a fork and refrigerate for 1 hour before filling.

Toasted Almond Crust

YIELD: **9-INCH PIECRUST (10 SERVINGS)**
PREP TIME: **5 MINUTES**
COOKING TIME: **15 MINUTES**

NUTRITIONAL INFO:
(PER SERVING)
CALORIES: **181**
NET CARBS: **3.2 G**
CARBS: **5.6 G**
FAT: **16.7 G**
PROTEIN: **4.8 G**
FIBER: **2.4 G**

INGREDIENTS

2 CUPS ALMOND FLOUR

⅓ CUP STEVIA OR PREFERRED
KETO-FRIENDLY SWEETENER

½ TEASPOON CINNAMON

½ TEASPOON KOSHER SALT

2¾ OZ. UNSALTED BUTTER,
MELTED

1 TO 3 TABLESPOONS ICE WATER

DIRECTIONS

1. Preheat the oven to 350°F. Place the almond flour in a skillet and toast over medium heat until it gives off a nutty aroma, 2 to 3 minutes. Transfer the flour to a mixing bowl and stir in the sweetener, cinnamon, and salt.

2. Incorporate the melted butter and work the mixture until it is coarse crumbs. Add the water incrementally if the mixture is too dry.

3. Place the mixture in a 9-inch pie plate and press it into the base and sides. Line with parchment paper and fill with rice or dried beans. Place in the oven and bake for 12 to 16 minutes, until the crust is dry to the touch and golden brown. Remove from the oven and let cool completely before filling.

Coffee & Chocolate Tart

YIELD: **3 SERVINGS**

PREP TIME: **5 MINUTES**

REFRIGERATION TIME:
1 HOUR AND 10 MINUTES

NUTRITIONAL INFO:
(PER SERVING)

CALORIES: **490**

NET CARBS: **3 G**

CARBS: **7 G**

FAT: **49 G**

PROTEIN: **8 G**

FIBER: **4 G**

INGREDIENTS

1½ OZ. ALMOND FLOUR

1 TEASPOON UNSWEETENED
COCOA POWDER

STEVIA OR PREFERRED KETO-
FRIENDLY SWEETENER, TO TASTE

1 TEASPOON PURE VANILLA
EXTRACT

2 TABLESPOONS SALTED BUTTER,
MELTED

1 TEASPOON INSTANT ESPRESSO
POWDER

2 TABLESPOONS HOT WATER (125°F)

5⅓ OZ. MASCARPONE CHEESE

3½ OZ. HEAVY CREAM

1 OZ. 85 PERCENT DARK
CHOCOLATE

COARSE SEA SALT, TO TASTE

DIRECTIONS

1. Preheat the oven to 350°F. Place the almond flour, cocoa powder, sweetener, vanilla, and butter in a mixing bowl and stir until the mixture has the consistency of wet sand.

2. Divide the mixture between three ramekins and press it into their bases. Bake for 10 minutes, remove from the oven, and let them cool slightly. Dissolve the instant espresso powder in the hot water and let it cool.

3. Place the mascarpone cheese, more sweetener, and the coffee in a bowl and beat until nice and fluffy. Pour the mascarpone mixture over the cooled tart bases and refrigerate for 10 minutes.

4. Microwave the heavy cream for 30 seconds. Add the chocolate and more sweetener and stir until you have a creamy ganache. Pour the ganache over the coffee-mascarpone crème and refrigerate for 1 hour.

5. Sprinkle sea salt over the tarts and serve.

Chocolate Fudge Tart

YIELD: **16 SERVINGS**
PREP TIME: **5 MINUTES**
COOKING TIME: **1 HOUR**

NUTRITIONAL INFO:
(PER SERVING)
CALORIES: **351**
NET CARBS: **10.5 G**
CARBS: **14.1 G**
FAT: **32 G**
PROTEIN: **5.8 G**
FIBER: **3.6 G**

INGREDIENTS

8 OZ. SUGAR-FREE BITTERSWEET CHOCOLATE, CHOPPED

1 STICK OF UNSALTED BUTTER

2 LARGE EGGS

1 CUP HEAVY CREAM

⅓ CUP STEVIA OR PREFERRED KETO-FRIENDLY SWEETENER

1 TEASPOON PURE VANILLA EXTRACT

PINCH OF KOSHER SALT

1 TART PASTRY SHELL
(SEE PAGE 131)

¼ CUP UNSWEETENED COCOA POWDER

DIRECTIONS

1. Preheat the oven to 350°F. Place the chocolate and butter in a small saucepan and cook over low heat, stirring frequently, until melted. Remove the pan from heat and set it aside.

2. In a large bowl, whisk together the eggs, cream, sweetener, vanilla, and salt. Stir in the chocolate mixture, spoon the filling into the tart shell, and gently shake the pan to evenly distribute.

3. Place the tart in the oven and bake for 15 to 20 minutes, until the filling is set around the edges but still soft in the center. Remove from the oven and let cool completely before sprinkling the cocoa powder over the top, slicing, and serving.

Raspberry & Mascarpone Tarts

YIELD: **6 SERVINGS**
PREP TIME: **20 MINUTES**
COOKING TIME: **10 MINUTES**

NUTRITIONAL INFO:
(PER SERVING)
CALORIES: **456**
NET CARBS: **5.3 G**
CARBS: **10.5 G**
FAT: **43.3 G**
PROTEIN: **8.5 G**
FIBER: **5.2 G**

INGREDIENTS

FOR THE CRUSTS

4 TABLESPOONS UNSALTED
BUTTER, MELTED AND COOLED,
PLUS MORE AS NEEDED

2 CUPS ALMOND FLOUR

¼ CUP GRANULATED ERYTHRITOL

½ TEASPOON KOSHER SALT

FOR THE FILLING

6 OZ. MASCARPONE CHEESE

3 TABLESPOONS GRANULATED
ERYTHRITOL

⅓ CUP HEAVY CREAM

2 TEASPOONS ORANGE ZEST

4 OZ. FRESH RASPBERRIES

DIRECTIONS

1. Preheat the oven to 350°F and grease six 4-inch tart pans with butter. To prepare the crusts, place all of the ingredients in a mixing bowl and stir until well combined. Press the mixture into the tart pans, place them in the oven, and bake for about 8 minutes, until they start to brown. Remove and let cool on wire racks before removing the crusts from the pans.

2. To prepare the filling, place the mascarpone and erythritol in a mixing bowl and beat with a handheld mixer until fluffy. Gradually add the cream and beat until incorporated. Stir in the orange zest, divide the mixture between the crusts, and top each tart with some of the raspberries.

NOTE: Do not fill the tarts more than 1 hour prior to serving.

Berry Cheesecake Tarts

YIELD: **8 SERVINGS**
PREP TIME: **15 MINUTES**
COOKING TIME: **30 MINUTES**

NUTRITIONAL INFO:
(PER SERVING)
CALORIES: **211**
NET CARBS: **6.5 G**
CARBS: **7.8 G**
FAT: **19.4 G**
PROTEIN: **5 G**
FIBER: **1.3 G**

INGREDIENTS

⅔ CUP ALMOND FLOUR

3 TABLESPOONS UNSALTED
BUTTER, MELTED AND COOLED

⅓ CUP GRANULATED ERYTHRITOL

PINCH OF CINNAMON

8 OZ. CREAM CHEESE, AT ROOM
TEMPERATURE

1 LARGE EGG

½ TEASPOON PURE VANILLA
EXTRACT

2 TEASPOONS FRESH LEMON JUICE

1 TEASPOON LEMON ZEST

¼ CUP SUGAR-FREE BLUEBERRY
JAM

0.8 OZ. FRESH BLUEBERRIES

DIRECTIONS

1. Preheat the oven to 350°F and line eight wells of a muffin tin with paper wrappers. Place the almond flour, butter, 2 tablespoons of the erythritol, and the cinnamon in a small bowl and stir to combine. Divide the mixture between the paper wrappers and use the back of a spoon to tamp it down.

2. Place in the oven and bake for 5 to 7 minutes, until the crusts are browned. Remove and let the crusts cool. Leave the oven on.

3. Place the cream cheese, egg, vanilla, lemon juice, lemon zest, and remaining erythritol in a mixing bowl and beat with a handheld mixer until light and fluffy. Spoon the filling into the crusts.

4. Place in the oven and bake the tarts for 20 minutes, until the filling is set. Remove and let cool for 10 minutes. Top each tart with a dollop of the jam and a few blueberries. Refrigerate until cold.

Avocado & Lime Tart

YIELD: **12 SERVINGS**
PREP TIME: **10 MINUTES**
REFRIGERATION TIME: **24 HOURS**

NUTRITIONAL INFO:
(PER SERVING)
CALORIES: **270**
NET CARBS: **4.9 G**
CARBS: **10.5 G**
FAT: **25 G**
PROTEIN: **5.2 G**
FIBER: **5.6 G**

INGREDIENTS

FLESH OF 4 AVOCADOS

JUICE OF 4 LIMES

¼ CUP STEVIA OR PREFERRED
KETO-FRIENDLY SWEETENER

¼ CUP COCONUT MILK

2 TABLESPOONS COCONUT OIL,
MELTED

1 TART PASTRY SHELL
(SEE PAGE 131)

2 TABLESPOONS UNSWEETENED
SHREDDED COCONUT

LIME SLICES, FOR GARNISH

DIRECTIONS

1. Place the avocados, lime juice, sweetener, coconut milk, and coconut oil in a food processor and puree until smooth.

2. Pour the filling into the pastry shell, cover with plastic wrap, and chill overnight. Top the tart with the coconut and lime slices before serving.

Honey & Buttermilk Pie

YIELD: **12 SERVINGS**
PREP TIME: **10 MINUTES**
REFRIGERATION TIME: **24 HOURS**

NUTRITIONAL INFO:
(PER SERVING)
CALORIES: **311**
NET CARBS: **10.7 G**
CARBS: **13.2 G**
FAT: **26.3 G**
PROTEIN: **8 G**
FIBER: **2.5 G**

INGREDIENTS

⅓ CUP STEVIA OR PREFERRED KETO-FRIENDLY SWEETENER

¾ CUP SOUR CREAM

⅔ CUP SUGAR-FREE HONEY SUBSTITUTE

¾ CUP BUTTERMILK

5 TABLESPOONS UNSALTED BUTTER, MELTED AND COOLED

2 TEASPOONS PURE VANILLA EXTRACT

½ TEASPOON CINNAMON

4 LARGE EGGS, LIGHTLY BEATEN

1 PERFECT PIECRUST, BLIND BAKED (SEE PAGES 132 AND 131, RESPECTIVELY)

¾ CUP LIGHT CREAM, CHILLED

DIRECTIONS

1. Preheat the oven to 300°F. Place the sweetener in a food processor and pulse until fine and powdery. Place it in a mixing bowl, add the eggs, and beat with a handheld mixer until thick and smooth. Add all of the remaining ingredients, except for the crust and the cream, and stir until the mixture is smooth and thoroughly combined.

2. Strain the mixture into the crust, place the pie in the oven, and bake for about 50 minutes, until the filling is set. Remove and let cool completely on a wire rack. Cover with plastic wrap and refrigerate overnight.

3. To serve, brown the top of the pie with a kitchen torch. Slice and drizzle some of the cream over each serving.

Peanut Butter Pie

YIELD: **12 SERVINGS**
PREP TIME: **10 MINUTES**
COOKING TIME: **1 HOUR**

NUTRITIONAL INFORMATION:
(PER SERVING)
CALORIES: **367**
NET CARBS: **10.2 G**
CARBS: **13.6 G**
FAT: **32.3 G**
PROTEIN: **11.1 G**
FIBER: **3.4 G**

INGREDIENTS

4 LARGE EGGS

½ CUP GRANULATED ERYTHRITOL

1 LB. NATURAL, NO SUGAR ADDED
PEANUT BUTTER

½ CUP HEAVY CREAM

1 TEASPOON PURE VANILLA
EXTRACT

1 TOASTED ALMOND CRUST
(SEE PAGE 135)

3½ OZ. SUGAR-FREE SEMISWEET
CHOCOLATE CHIPS

DIRECTIONS

1. Preheat the oven to 350°F. Place the eggs and erythritol
    in a mixing bowl and beat with a handheld mixer until the
    sweetener has dissolved. Add the peanut butter, cream,
    and vanilla and beating until thoroughly incorporated.

2. Pour the mixture into the crust and smooth the top with
    a rubber spatula. Place in the oven and bake for about
    1 hour, until a knife inserted into the center comes out
    clean. Remove from the oven and let cool.

3. Place the chocolate chips in a microwave-safe bowl and
    microwave on medium until melted, about 10 seconds.
    Let the melted chocolate cool for 5 minutes and then
    spread it over the top of the pie. Refrigerate until the
    chocolate is set, about 1 hour.

Pecan Pie

YIELD: **12 SERVINGS**
PREP TIME: **20 MINUTES**
COOKING TIME: **45 MINUTES**

NUTRITIONAL INFORMATION:
(PER SERVING)
CALORIES: **541**
NET CARBS: **5.7 G**
CARBS: **10.2 G**
FAT: **54.6 G**
PROTEIN: **7.6 G**
FIBER: **4.5 G**

INGREDIENTS

1½ STICKS OF UNSALTED BUTTER,
PLUS MORE AS NEEDED

¾ CUP GRANULATED ERYTHRITOL

1½ CUPS HEAVY CREAM

1 TEASPOON FLAKY SEA SALT

2 TEASPOONS PURE VANILLA
EXTRACT

1 PERFECT PIECRUST
(SEE PAGE 132)

ALMOND FLOUR, AS NEEDED

1 LARGE EGG, AT ROOM
TEMPERATURE

11 OZ. PECAN HALVES

DIRECTIONS

1. Preheat the oven to 350°F and grease a 9-inch pie plate with butter. Place the butter and the erythritol in a saucepan and cook over medium heat, stirring occasionally, until it is melted, about 5 minutes.

2. Stir in the cream and salt and simmer the mixture until it is thick and a dark golden brown about 15 minutes. Remove from heat and stir in the vanilla extract.

3. Place the piecrust on a flour-dusted work surface and roll it out to fit the pie plate. Place the crust in the pie plate, prick the bottom with a fork, and refrigerate it for 15 minutes.

4. Add the egg to the caramel and stir to combine. Place the pecans in the piecrust and pour the caramel over them.

5. Place the pie in the oven and bake for about 45 minutes, until the filling is set. Remove from the oven and let cool before serving.

CHAPTER 4

FROZEN DELIGHTS

Cakes and cookies have the most fans, but when it comes down to it, all desserts take a back seat to ice cream. Sweet, luxurious, and refreshing, it has everything someone in need of a treat at the end of a long day could possibly want. The keto-friendly iterations in this category are no different. From the classic flavors of chocolate and vanilla to bold, innovative flavors like avocado and matcha, there's no shortage of options for the ice cream obsessive. There's also a few other frozen treats, like Root Beer Floats (see page 169) or Raspberry Cheesecake Pops (see page 185), to cool you down when the temperature starts to rise.

Chocolate Ice Cream

YIELD: **6 SERVINGS**

PREP TIME: **5 MINUTES**

FREEZING TIME: **4 HOURS**

NUTRITIONAL INFO:
(PER SERVING)

CALORIES: **311**

NET CARBS: **6.8 G**

CARBS: **9.2 G**

FAT: **29.6 G**

PROTEIN: **5.2 G**

FIBER: **2.4 G**

INGREDIENTS

1½ CUPS HEAVY CREAM

¾ CUP WHOLE MILK

¼ CUP UNSWEETENED COCOA POWDER

½ CUP STEVIA OR PREFERRED KETO-FRIENDLY SWEETENER

3 LARGE EGG YOLKS, LIGHTLY BEATEN

1¾ OZ. BAKER'S CHOCOLATE, CHOPPED

½ TEASPOON PURE VANILLA EXTRACT

PINCH OF FLAKY SEA SALT

1½ TABLESPOONS VODKA (OPTIONAL)

DIRECTIONS

1. Prepare an ice bath in a large bowl. Place the cream, ½ cup of the milk, the cocoa powder, and sweetener in a saucepan and warm over medium heat while stirring. Once the sugar has dissolved, take approximately 1 cup from the mixture in the saucepan and whisk it into the bowl containing the egg yolks. Add the tempered eggs to the saucepan and continue cooking over medium heat until the contents have thickened to where they will coat the back of a wooden spoon. Remove the pan from heat.

2. Stir the chocolate into the custard, let the mixture cool for 5 minutes, and then stir until it is smooth. Pour the custard into a bowl and then set the bowl in the ice bath. Stir occasionally until the mixture is smooth, about 10 minutes. Cover the bowl with plastic wrap and refrigerate for 3 hours.

3. Stir in the remaining milk, the vanilla, salt, and vodka (if using). Pour the mixture into an ice cream maker and churn until the mixture has the desired consistency, about 20 minutes. Pour into an airtight container, cover, and freeze until firm, about 4 hours.

TIP: Using the vodka will help prevent the formation of ice crystals in the ice cream, ultimately yielding a smoother texture.

Vanilla Ice Cream

YIELD: **8 SERVINGS**
PREP TIME: **5 MINUTES**
FREEZING TIME: **4 HOURS**

NUTRITIONAL INFO:
(PER SERVING)
CALORIES: **312**
NET CARBS: **2.9 G**
CARBS: **2.9 G**
FAT: **32.7 G**
PROTEIN: **1.5 G**
FIBER: **0 G**

INGREDIENTS

¼ CUP STEVIA OR PREFERRED KETO-FRIENDLY SWEETENER

2 TABLESPOONS UNSALTED BUTTER

2½ CUPS HEAVY CREAM

SEEDS OF 1 VANILLA BEAN

2 TABLESPOONS MCT OIL

2 TEASPOONS PURE VANILLA EXTRACT

DIRECTIONS

1. Place the sweetener in a food processor and pulse until fine and powdery.

2. Place the butter in a saucepan and melt over medium heat. Whisk in 1⅔ cups of the cream and the sweetener, bring to a simmer, and cook until reduced by half, about 25 minutes. Pour the mixture into a bowl and let it cool to room temperature.

3. Whisk in the vanilla seeds, MCT oil, vanilla extract, and the remaining cream. Cover and refrigerate for 4 hours.

4. Pour the mixture into an ice cream maker and churn until the desired consistency has been achieved, about 20 minutes. Transfer to an airtight container, cover, and freeze for 4 hours before serving.

Vegan Vanilla Ice Cream

YIELD: **6 SERVINGS**
PREP TIME: **5 MINUTES**
FREEZING TIME: **4 HOURS**

NUTRITIONAL INFO:
(PER SERVING)
CALORIES: **188**
NET CARBS: **1.1 G**
CARBS: **1.1 G**
FAT: **18.8 G**
PROTEIN: **1.6 G**
FIBER: **0 G**

INGREDIENTS

¼ CUP STEVIA OR PREFERRED KETO-FRIENDLY SWEETENER

2 TABLESPOONS COCONUT OIL

2½ CUPS COCONUT MILK

SEEDS AND POD OF 1 VANILLA BEAN

2 TABLESPOONS MCT OIL

2 TEASPOONS PURE VANILLA EXTRACT

DIRECTIONS

1. Place the sweetener in a food processor and pulse until fine and powdery.

2. Place the coconut oil in a saucepan and warm over medium heat. Whisk in 1⅔ cups of the coconut milk and the sweetener. Bring to a simmer and cook until reduced by half, about 25 minutes. Pour into a bowl, stir in the vanilla seeds and pod, and let it cool to room temperature.

3. Whisk in the MCT oil, vanilla extract, and the remaining coconut milk. Cover the bowl and refrigerate for 4 hours.

4. Discard the vanilla bean pod, pour the mixture into an ice cream maker, and churn until the desired consistency has been achieved, about 20 minutes. Transfer to an airtight container, cover, and freeze for 4 hours before serving.

Hot Fudge Sundaes

YIELD: **6 SERVINGS**
PREP TIME: **5 MINUTES**
COOKING TIME: **N/A**

NUTRITIONAL INFO:
(PER SERVING)
CALORIES: **712**
NET CARBS: **7.2 G**
CARBS: **9 G**
FAT: **75.2 G**
PROTEIN: **4.9 G**
FIBER: **1.8 G**

INGREDIENTS

1 CUP HOT FUDGE (SEE SIDEBAR)

2 CUPS VANILLA ICE CREAM
(SEE PAGE 158)

1 CUP WHIPPED CREAM
(SEE PAGE 238)

1½ OZ. PECAN HALVES, CHOPPED
(OPTIONAL)

6 LUXARDO MARASCHINO
CHERRIES (OPTIONAL)

DIRECTIONS

1. Divide the Hot Fudge between six bowls or tulip sundae dishes.

2. Scoop the ice cream into the bowls and top with Whipped Cream. Add the pecans and/or maraschino cherries, if desired, and serve immediately.

HOT FUDGE

Place 1 cup heavy cream and ⅓ cup Swerve Confectioners' in a saucepan, whisk to combine, and bring to a simmer over medium heat. Remove the saucepan from heat, stir in 2¾ oz. sugar-free semisweet chocolate chips, and let the mixture sit until they have melted. Whisk in ½ teaspoon vanilla and a pinch of kosher salt and stir until the mixture is smooth. This preparation will result in 8 servings of hot fudge. The macros per serving are as follows: 132 calories, 1.6 grams net carbs, 2.5 grams carbs, 13.9 grams fat, 1.3 grams protein, and 0.9 grams fiber.

Easy Strawberry Ice Cream

YIELD: **6 SERVINGS**

PREP TIME: **5 MINUTES**

FREEZING TIME: **4 HOURS**

NUTRITIONAL INFO:
(PER SERVING)

CALORIES: **320**

NET CARBS: **4.5 G**

CARBS: **4.9 G**

FAT: **33 G**

PROTEIN: **2 G**

FIBER: **0.4 G**

INGREDIENTS

2 CUPS HEAVY CREAM

5¼ OZ. HULLED AND SLICED STRAWBERRIES

⅓ CUP STEVIA OR PREFERRED KETO-FRIENDLY SWEETENER

2 TABLESPOONS CRÈME FRAÎCHE

1 TEASPOON PURE VANILLA EXTRACT

DIRECTIONS

1. Place all of the ingredients in a food processor and puree until smooth. Pour the mixture into a square 8-inch cake pan, making sure it is evenly distributed.

2. Cover and freeze for about 4 hours, until the ice cream is firm but not rock-solid.

Classic Vanilla Milkshakes

YIELD: **4 SERVINGS**
PREP TIME: **5 MINUTES**
COOKING TIME: **5 MINUTES**

NUTRITIONAL INFO:
(PER SERVING)
CALORIES: **349**
NET CARBS: **5.7 G**
CARBS: **5.7 G**
FAT: **34.7 G**
PROTEIN: **3.5 G**
FIBER: **0 G**

INGREDIENTS

2 CUPS VANILLA ICE CREAM
(SEE PAGE 158)

1 CUP WHOLE MILK

½ TEASPOON KOSHER SALT

2 TEASPOONS PURE VANILLA
EXTRACT

4 SPRIGS OF FRESH MINT, FOR
GARNISH

DIRECTIONS

1. Place the ice cream, milk, salt, and vanilla in a blender
    and puree until smooth.

2. Pour into glasses and garnish each shake with a sprig
    of mint.

Root Beer Floats

YIELD: **4 SERVINGS**
PREP TIME: **5 MINUTES**
COOKING TIME: **N/A**

NUTRITIONAL INFO:
(PER SERVING)
CALORIES: **415**
NET CARBS: **3.7 G**
CARBS: **3.7 G**
FAT: **43.8 G**
PROTEIN: **2.1 G**
FIBER: **0 G**

INGREDIENTS

2 CUPS VANILLA ICE CREAM
(SEE PAGE 158)

4 (12 OZ.) BOTTLES OF SUGAR-FREE
ROOT BEER, CHILLED

1 CUP WHIPPED CREAM
(SEE PAGE 238)

DIRECTIONS

1. Divide the ice cream between four glasses. Slowly pour root beer into each glass and top each serving with some of the Whipped Cream.

Coconut Ice Cream

YIELD: **6 SERVINGS**
PREP TIME: **5 MINUTES**
FREEZING TIME: **4 HOURS**

NUTRITIONAL INFO:
(PER SERVING)
CALORIES: **355**
NET CARBS: **5.5 G**
CARBS: **5.5 G**
FAT: **36 G**
PROTEIN: **2.7 G**
FIBER: **0 G**

INGREDIENTS

1⅔ CUPS COCONUT MILK

⅔ CUP STEVIA OR PREFERRED
KETO-FRIENDLY SWEETENER

1 TEASPOON PURE VANILLA
EXTRACT

2 TEASPOONS COCONUT EXTRACT

PINCH OF KOSHER SALT

¾ TEASPOON ARROWROOT STARCH

1 TABLESPOON WATER

2 CUPS HEAVY CREAM

DIRECTIONS

1. Place the coconut milk, sweetener, extracts, and salt in a saucepan and cook over medium heat, stirring frequently, until the sweetener has dissolved. Combine the arrowroot starch and water in a bowl, stir the slurry into the saucepan, and simmer until the mixture is smooth, 2 to 3 minutes.

2. Working over a mixing bowl, strain the mixture through a fine sieve, press a piece of plastic wrap directly on the surface, and refrigerate for 2 hours.

3. Place the cream in a mixing bowl and beat until it holds soft peaks. Fold in the coconut milk mixture, transfer to an ice cream maker, and churn until the mixture is the desired consistency, about 20 minutes. Transfer to an airtight container, cover, and freeze for 4 hours before serving. If you're looking for a little something to top this ice cream with, whip up some of the Caramel on the opposite page.

CARAMEL

Place 4 tablespoons unsalted butter in a saucepan and cook, while stirring, until it has browned and gives off a nutty aroma, 4 to 5 minutes. Stir in ⅓ cup stevia or your preferred keto-friendly sweetener, ½ cup heavy cream, and ⅔ teaspoon kosher salt, reduce heat to the lowest possible setting, and cook, while stirring occasionally, until the caramel has thickened to the desired consistency, 12 to 15 minutes. Remove the pan from heat, stir in ½ teaspoon pure vanilla extract, and use immediately. This preparation will yield 8 servings of caramel. The macros for each serving are as follows: 106 calories, 1.3 grams net carbs, 1.3 grams carbs, 11 grams fat, 0.3 grams protein, and 0 grams fiber

Vegan Turmeric Ice Cream

YIELD: **4 SERVINGS**
PREP TIME: **5 MINUTES**
FREEZING TIME: **4 HOURS**

NUTRITIONAL INFO:
(PER SERVING)
CALORIES: **220**
NET CARBS: **1.9 G**
CARBS: **2.6 G**
FAT: **21 G**
PROTEIN: **4 G**
FIBER: **0.7 G**

INGREDIENTS

2⅓ CUPS COCONUT MILK

¼ CUP STEVIA OR PREFERRED KETO-FRIENDLY SWEETENER

PINCH OF KOSHER SALT

1½ TEASPOONS TURMERIC

¼ TEASPOON CINNAMON

¼ TEASPOON CARDAMOM

1 TEASPOON PURE VANILLA EXTRACT

1½ TABLESPOONS OLIVE OIL

1 TABLESPOON HEMP HEARTS, FOR GARNISH

DIRECTIONS

1. Prepare an ice bath in a large bowl. Place the coconut milk, sweetener, salt, spices, and vanilla in a saucepan and bring to a simmer over medium heat, while whisking constantly. When the sugar has dissolved and the mixture is smooth, pour it into a mixing bowl and set the bowl in the ice bath. Stir occasionally until the mixture is cold to the touch.

2. Stir in the olive oil, pour the mixture into an ice cream maker, and churn until the desired consistency has been achieved, about 20 minutes. Pour the ice cream into an airtight container, cover, and freeze for 4 hours. To serve, let the ice cream sit at room temperature for 5 minutes and then sprinkle the hemp hearts over each serving.

Lavender Ice Cream

YIELD: **8 SERVINGS**
PREP TIME: **5 MINUTES**
FREEZING TIME: **4 HOURS**

NUTRITIONAL INFORMATION:
(PER SERVING)
CALORIES: **310**
NET CARBS: **2.8 G**
CARBS: **2.8 G**
FAT: **32.7 G**
PROTEIN: **1.5 G**
FIBER: **0 G**

INGREDIENTS

2 TABLESPOONS UNSALTED BUTTER

2½ CUPS HEAVY CREAM

¼ CUP POWDERED ERYTHRITOL

2 TABLESPOONS MCT OIL

1½ TEASPOONS PURE LAVENDER
EXTRACT

½ TEASPOON PURE VANILLA
EXTRACT

DIRECTIONS

1. Place the butter in a saucepan and melt it over a medium heat. Stir in three-quarters of the cream and the powdered erythritol and bring to a simmer. Cook until the mixture has reduced by half, about 25 minutes. Pour the mixture into a bowl and let it cool to room temperature.

2. Stir in the MCT oil, extracts, and the remaining cream. Cover the bowl with plastic wrap and refrigerate for 4 hours.

3. Pour the mixture into an ice cream maker and churn until the it has the desired consistency, about 20 minutes. Place in an airtight container, cover, and freeze until firm, about 4 hours.

Matcha Ice Cream

YIELD: **4 SERVINGS**
PREP TIME: **5 MINUTES**
FREEZING TIME: **4 HOURS**

NUTRITIONAL INFO:
(PER SERVING)
CALORIES: **294**
NET CARBS: **1.7 G**
CARBS: **4.5 G**
FAT: **27.5 G**
PROTEIN: **7.9 G**
FIBER: **2.8 G**

INGREDIENTS

2 TABLESPOONS MATCHA POWDER

1 CUP UNSWEETENED ALMOND MILK

1 CUP HEAVY CREAM

⅓ CUP STEVIA OR PREFERRED KETO-FRIENDLY SWEETENER

2 LARGE EGGS

1 LARGE EGG YOLK

1 TEASPOON PURE VANILLA EXTRACT

DIRECTIONS

1. Prepare an ice bath in a large bowl. Place the matcha powder and almond milk in a mixing bowl and stir to combine. Stir in the cream and pour the mixture into a saucepan. Cook over medium heat, stirring frequently, until the mixture comes to a simmer.

2. Place the remaining ingredients in a heatproof bowl and beat with a handheld mixer until pale and thick. Gradually incorporate the mixture in the saucepan. When all of it has been incorporated, pour the resulting mixture into the saucepan, reduce the heat to medium-low, and cook until the mixture thickens enough to coat the back of a wooden spoon, 3 to 4 minutes.

3. Pour the custard into a bowl and place the bowl in the ice bath. Let it sit until it is cold, about 25 minutes, and stir the custard occasionally.

4. Place the custard in an ice cream machine and churn until the desired consistency has been achieved, about 20 minutes. Transfer to an airtight container, cover, and freeze for 4 hours before serving.

Avocado Ice Cream

YIELD: **4 SERVINGS**
PREP TIME: **5 MINUTES**
FREEZING TIME: **4 HOURS**

NUTRITIONAL INFO:
(PER SERVING)
CALORIES: **259**
NET CARBS: **3 G**
CARBS: **9.2 G**
FAT: **24.5 G**
PROTEIN: **2.9 G**
FIBER: **6.2 G**

INGREDIENTS

FLESH OF 2 AVOCADOS

1 CUP COCONUT MILK

1 TABLESPOON FRESH LEMON
JUICE

1 TABLESPOON MCT OIL

2 TABLESPOONS STEVIA OR
PREFERRED KETO-FRIENDLY
SWEETENER

PINCH OF KOSHER SALT

UNSWEETENED COCONUT FLAKES,
TOASTED, FOR GARNISH

DIRECTIONS

1. Place the avocados, coconut milk, lemon juice, MCT oil, sweetener, and salt in a food processor and puree until smooth, scraping down the sides of the work bowl as needed.

2. Transfer the mixture to an ice cream machine and churn until the desired consistency has been achieved, about 20 minutes. Transfer the mixture to an airtight container, cover, and freeze for 4 hours. To serve, garnish each portion with some coconut.

MCT OIL

MCT oil is a dietary supplement that is made up of medium-chain triglycerides, meaning they are composed of chains of 6 to 12 carbon atoms. They are processed differently than other fats, going straight from the gut to the liver, where they are turned into the ketones that the ketogenic diet aims to produce.

Frozen Lemon Mousse

YIELD: **6 SERVINGS**
PREP TIME: **15 MINUTES**
FREEZING TIME: **2 HOURS**

NUTRITIONAL INFO:
(PER SERVING)
CALORIES: **244**
NET CARBS: **2.6 G**
CARBS: **2.6 G**
FAT: **24.4 G**
PROTEIN: **4.4 G**
FIBER: **0 G**

INGREDIENTS

3 LARGE EGGS, YOLKS AND WHITES
SEPARATED

¼ TEASPOON CREAM OF TARTAR

PINCH OF KOSHER SALT

½ CUP GRANULATED ERYTHRITOL

ZEST AND JUICE OF 1 LEMON

1½ CUPS HEAVY CREAM

DIRECTIONS

1. Place the egg whites in a mixing bowl and beat with a handheld mixer until frothy. Add the cream of tartar and salt and beat until the mixture holds stiff peaks.

2. Place the egg yolks in a separate bowl and beat until thick. Gradually add the erythritol and beat until incorporated. Stir in the lemon zest and lemon juice and then fold the yolk mixture into the meringue.

3. Place the cream in a chilled mixing bowl and beat with chilled beaters until soft peaks form. Fold the whipped cream into the mousse. Freeze the mousse for at least 2 hours, while stirring every 30 minutes. To serve, let the mousse sit at room temperature for 10 minutes before scooping it into the serving dishes.

Blackberry Frozen Yogurt

YIELD: **4 SERVINGS**
PREP TIME: **5 MINUTES**
FREEZING TIME: **3 HOURS**

NUTRITIONAL INFO:
(PER SERVING)
CALORIES: **195**
NET CARBS: **8.1 G**
CARBS: **9.4 G**
FAT: **11.9 G**
PROTEIN: **10.3 G**
FIBER: **1.3 G**

INGREDIENTS

1½ CUPS PLAIN GREEK YOGURT

½ CUP WHOLE MILK

½ CUP HEAVY CREAM

¼ CUP SUGAR-FREE WHEY PROTEIN
(PLAIN OR VANILLA)

3 TABLESPOONS STEVIA OR
PREFERRED KETO-FRIENDLY
SWEETENER

4 OZ. BLACKBERRIES, RINSED

DIRECTIONS

1. Place the yogurt, milk, cream, whey protein, and sweetener in a large mixing bowl and stir until the sweetener and whey protein have dissolved.

2. Puree the blackberries in a food processor, strain the puree through a fine sieve into the yogurt mixture, and discard the seeds. Stir the mixture until thoroughly combined.

3. Pour the mixture into an ice cream maker and churn until the desired consistency has been achieved, about 20 minutes. Transfer to an airtight container, cover, and freeze for 3 hours before serving.

Raspberry Cheesecake Pops

YIELD: **6 SERVINGS**
PREP TIME: **5 MINUTES**
FREEZING TIME: **4 HOURS**

NUTRITIONAL INFO:
(PER SERVING)
CALORIES: **249**
NET CARBS: **9 G**
CARBS: **11.4 G**
FAT: **21.1 G**
PROTEIN: **5.5 G**
FIBER: **2.4 G**

INGREDIENTS

½ CUP ALMOND FLOUR

3 TABLESPOONS COCONUT OIL, MELTED

1½ TABLESPOONS STEVIA OR PREFERRED KETO-FRIENDLY SWEETENER, PLUS ¼ CUP

1 TEASPOON PURE VANILLA EXTRACT

⅓ CUP HEAVY CREAM

4 OZ. RASPBERRIES

2 CUPS PLAIN GREEK YOGURT

6 POPSICLE STICKS

DIRECTIONS

1. Preheat the oven to 350°F and grease a 9 x 5-inch loaf pan with nonstick cooking spray. Place the almond flour, coconut oil, 1½ tablespoons of sweetener, and vanilla in a small mixing bowl and stir until combined. Press the mixture into the loaf pan, place in the oven, and bake until golden brown and set, about 12 to 15 minutes. Remove from the oven, place on a wire rack, and let cool completely.

2. Break the baked crust into pieces. Place the remaining sweetener, the cream, and raspberries in a food processor and puree until smooth. Working over a mixing bowl, strain the puree through a fine sieve. Stir in the pieces of crust and yogurt, pour the mixture into silicone popsicle molds, and freeze for 45 minutes.

3. Insert the popsicle sticks, return to the freezer, and freeze for another 3 hours and 15 minutes before serving.

Frozen Fruit Bars

YIELD: **6 SERVINGS**
PREP TIME: **5 MINUTES**
FREEZING TIME: **4 HOURS**

NUTRITIONAL INFO:
(PER SERVING)
CALORIES: **284**
NET CARBS: **5.1 G**
CARBS: **6.6 G**
FAT: **28 G**
PROTEIN: **2.7 G**
FIBER: **1.5 G**

INGREDIENTS

1¼ CUPS HEAVY CREAM

1¼ CUPS LIGHT CREAM

1 TEASPOON PURE VANILLA
EXTRACT

4 LARGE EGG YOLKS

2 TABLESPOONS STEVIA OR
PREFERRED KETO-FRIENDLY
SWEETENER

4 OZ. FROZEN RASPBERRIES

6 POPSICLE STICKS

DIRECTIONS

1. Place the creams in a saucepan and bring to a simmer over medium heat. Remove from heat, stir in the vanilla, and let the mixture sit for 5 minutes.

2. Place the egg yolks and sweetener in a heatproof bowl and beat until pale and thick. Gradually whisk the vanilla cream into the egg mixture and stir until thoroughly combined. Strain the mixture into a clean saucepan and cook over low heat, stirring constantly, until it is thick enough to coat the back of a wooden spoon.

3. Pour the custard into a large bowl, place plastic wrap directly on the surface, and refrigerate for 2 hours.

4. Place the raspberries in a food processor and pulse until crushed. Fold them into the chilled custard and pour the mixture into silicone popsicle molds. Place in the freezer for 1 hour, remove, and insert the popsicle sticks. Freeze for another 3 hours before serving.

Strawberry Creamsicles

YIELD: **6 SERVINGS**
PREP TIME: **5 MINUTES**
FREEZING TIME: **4 HOURS**

NUTRITIONAL INFO:
(PER SERVING)
CALORIES: **138**
NET CARBS: **8.7 G**
CARBS: **9.5 G**
FAT: **10.9 G**
PROTEIN: **2.8 G**
FIBER: **0.8 G**

INGREDIENTS

10½ OZ. FROZEN STRAWBERRIES

1½ CUPS PLAIN GREEK YOGURT

½ CUP HEAVY CREAM

2 TEASPOONS SWERVE CONFECTIONERS'

1 TEASPOON PURE VANILLA EXTRACT

6 POPSICLE STICKS

DIRECTIONS

1. Place the strawberries in a bowl and let them thaw for 15 minutes. Place the strawberries, yogurt, cream, sweetener, and vanilla in a food processor and puree until smooth. Pour the mixture into silicone popsicle molds and freeze for 1 hour.

2. Remove the popsicles from the freezer, insert the popsicle sticks, and freeze for another 3 hours before serving.

Black Currant Ice Cream Cake

YIELD: **12 SERVINGS**
PREP TIME: **10 MINUTES**
FREEZING TIME: **5 HOURS**

NUTRITIONAL INFO:
(PER SERVING)
CALORIES: **325**
NET CARBS: **6.3 G**
CARBS: **8.7 G**
FAT: **30.6 G**
PROTEIN: **6.9 G**
FIBER: **2.4 G**

INGREDIENTS

FOR THE ICE CREAM

5 OZ. BLACK CURRANTS, STEMMED

½ CUP STEVIA OR PREFERRED
KETO-FRIENDLY SWEETENER, PLUS
2 TABLESPOONS

1¼ CUPS HEAVY CREAM

1¼ CUPS WHOLE MILK

8 OZ. CREAM CHEESE, AT ROOM
TEMPERATURE

½ TEASPOON PURE VANILLA
EXTRACT

PINCH OF KOSHER SALT

FOR THE CAKE

2 CUPS ALMOND FLOUR

5 TABLESPOONS UNSALTED
BUTTER, MELTED

3 TABLESPOONS STEVIA OR
PREFERRED KETO-FRIENDLY
SWEETENER

1 TEASPOON PURE VANILLA
EXTRACT

DIRECTIONS

1. To begin preparations for the ice cream, place the black currants, 2 tablespoons of sweetener, and a splash of water in a saucepan, cover the pan, and cook over medium heat, stirring occasionally, until the black currants soften and burst, about 10 minutes. Remove the pan from heat, let cool briefly, and then transfer the mixture to a bowl. Store in the refrigerator.

2. Place the cream, milk, cream cheese, ½ cup of sweetener, vanilla, and salt in a food processor and pulse until the sweetener has dissolved. Pour the mixture into an ice cream maker and churn for 15 minutes. Add the black currant mixture and churn for another 5 minutes. Store the mixture in the freezer when it reaches the desired consistency.

3. While churning the ice cream, preheat the oven to 350°F. To prepare the cake, place all of the ingredients in a mixing bowl, stir to combine, and press the mixture into a springform pan. Place in the oven and bake for about 12 minutes, until golden brown and dry to the touch. Remove and let cool completely on a wire rack.

4. When the cake has cooled, spread the ice cream over it, cover the cake with plastic wrap, and freeze for 5 hours before serving.

Coffee Granita with Cream

YIELD: **4 SERVINGS**
PREP TIME: **5 MINUTES**
FREEZING TIME: **4 HOURS**

NUTRITIONAL INFO:
(PER SERVING)
CALORIES: **151**
NET CARBS: **7.4 G**
CARBS: **7.4 G**
FAT: **14 G**
PROTEIN: **1 G**
FIBER: **0 G**

INGREDIENTS

2½ CUPS BREWED COFFEE, AT ROOM TEMPERATURE

¼ CUP STEVIA OR PREFERRED KETO-FRIENDLY SWEETENER

½ TEASPOON CINNAMON

1 TEASPOON PURE VANILLA EXTRACT

⅔ CUP HEAVY CREAM

DIRECTIONS

1. Place the brewed coffee, sweetener, cinnamon, and vanilla in a square 8-inch cake pan and stir until the sweetener has dissolved. Place in the freezer and freeze for 1 hour.

2. Remove from the freezer and run a fork over the mixture to break up the texture. Return to the freezer and freeze for another 3 hours, removing to break up the granita with a fork every hour, until the granita is coarse in texture.

3. Place the cream in a mixing bowl and beat until it holds soft peaks. Divide the granita between the serving dishes and top each portion with some of the whipped cream.

CHAPTER 5

PUDDINGS, PARFAITS & BEVERAGES

Easy to prepare, making negligible impacts on your macros, and absolutely decadent, the offerings in this chapter are where you'll turn when your sweet tooth needs a quick fix. But make sure you take your time moving through this section, as it also contains difficult-to-categorize but stone-cold classics such as Eton Mess and Crème Brûlée (see pages 212 and 216, respectively).

Chocolate Pudding

YIELD: **6 SERVINGS**

PREP TIME: **5 MINUTES**

REFRIGERATION TIME: **2 HOURS**

NUTRITIONAL INFO:
(PER SERVING)

CALORIES: **153**

NET CARBS: **7 G**

CARBS: **9.6 G**

FAT: **12 G**

PROTEIN: **5.2 G**

FIBER: **2.6 G**

INGREDIENTS

¼ CUP STEVIA OR PREFERRED KETO-FRIENDLY SWEETENER

1¼ OZ. BAKER'S CHOCOLATE, CHOPPED

¼ CUP UNSWEETENED COCOA POWDER

¼ CUP ALMOND FLOUR

½ TEASPOON KOSHER SALT

2 CUPS WHOLE MILK

¼ CUP HEAVY CREAM

4 TABLESPOONS UNSALTED BUTTER, DIVIDED INTO TABLESPOONS

2 TEASPOONS PURE VANILLA EXTRACT

¾ OZ. UNSWEETENED SHREDDED COCONUT (OPTIONAL)

2½ OZ. RASPBERRIES (OPTIONAL)

1¼ OZ. SUGAR-FREE CHOCOLATE CHIPS, CHOPPED (OPTIONAL)

DIRECTIONS

1. Place the sweetener, chocolate, cocoa powder, almond flour, and salt in a saucepan and whisk to combine. Cook over medium heat and slowly add the milk while whisking constantly. Cook until the mixture thickens and comes to a boil, approximately 8 to 10 minutes.

2. Reduce the heat to low and simmer for 1 to 2 minutes. Remove the saucepan from heat and stir in the cream. Incorporate the butter 1 tablespoon at a time and then stir in the vanilla.

3. Transfer the pudding into the serving dishes and place plastic wrap directly on the pudding's surface to prevent a skin from forming. Refrigerate for 2 hours before serving and top with shredded coconut, raspberries, and/or chocolate chips, if desired.

Vanilla Pudding

YIELD: **4 SERVINGS**
PREP TIME: **5 MINUTES**
REFRIGERATION TIME: **2 HOURS**

NUTRITIONAL INFO:
(PER SERVING)
CALORIES: **491**
NET CARBS: **5.8 G**
CARBS: **5.8 G**
FAT: **49.7 G**
PROTEIN: **5.8 G**
FIBER: **0 G**

INGREDIENTS

2 CUPS HEAVY CREAM

SEEDS AND POD OF 1 VANILLA
BEAN

5 LARGE EGG YOLKS

⅓ CUP STEVIA OR PREFERRED
KETO-FRIENDLY SWEETENER

DIRECTIONS

1. Place the cream, vanilla seeds, and vanilla pod in a saucepan and warm over medium heat for 5 minutes. Remove from heat and let cool for 5 minutes.

2. Place the egg yolks and sweetener in a heatproof bowl and beat until pale and thick. Gradually incorporate ½ cup of the mixture in the saucepan and then pour the tempered egg yolks into the saucepan. Cook over medium-low heat, while stirring constantly, until the mixture is thick enough to coat the back of a wooden spoon. Strain the pudding into a bowl, press plastic wrap directly on the surface to prevent a skin from forming, and refrigerate for 2 hours before serving.

VARIETIES OF VANILLA

As those who are devotees of the vanilla bean know, there is plenty of variation within this flavor that many unfairly brand as bland. Here's a look at the varieties of vanilla beans and extracts you're most likely to encounter:

Madagascar Bourbon: These beans have nothing to do with American whiskey—though, to be fair, it's an understandable mistake given that many bourbons do carry strong notes of vanilla. Instead, it refers to Bourbon Island (now known as Reunion), an island east of Madagascar in the Indian Ocean after which the vanilla that grows in the region was named. The sweet, creamy flavor of these beans is what comes to mind when most think of vanilla, as its incredible versatility has made it ubiquitous.

Mexican: This vanilla adds a bit of nutmeg-y spice to the famously sweet and creamy quality. Because of this piquant quality, Mexican vanilla goes wonderfully with those cinnamon- and nutmeg-heavy desserts.

Indonesian: These beans carry a smoky, woody flavor and aroma that is particularly welcome in cookies and chocolate-rich desserts.

Tahitian: A fruity, floral flavor that carries hints of stone fruit and anise makes Tahitian vanilla a perfect match for fruit-based desserts, as well as ice creams and custards.

Vegan Rice Pudding

YIELD: **6 SERVINGS**
PREP TIME: **5 MINUTES**
COOKING TIME: **30 MINUTES**

NUTRITIONAL INFO:
(PER SERVING)
CALORIES: **149**
NET CARBS: **7.1 G**
CARBS: **9.1 G**
FAT: **11.4 G**
PROTEIN: **1.3 G**
FIBER: **2 G**

INGREDIENTS

7 OZ. KONJAC RICE

2 CUPS COCONUT MILK

⅓ CUP STEVIA OR PREFERRED KETO-FRIENDLY GRANULATED SWEETENER

¼ TEASPOON KOSHER SALT

SEEDS AND POD OF 1 VANILLA BEAN

1 CINNAMON STICK

1½ TABLESPOONS COCONUT OIL

1 TEASPOON GRATED FRESH NUTMEG, FOR GARNISH

DIRECTIONS

1. Rinse the rice under cold water for 2 minutes and then let it drain. Bring water to a boil in a saucepan, add the konjac rice, and cook for 3 minutes. Drain and transfer to a clean saucepan. Add 1½ cups of the coconut milk, the sweetener, salt, vanilla seeds and pod, and the cinnamon stick and cook over medium heat, stirring occasionally, until the mixture has thickened, about 20 minutes.

2. Remove from heat and stir in the remaining coconut milk. Return over medium heat and cook, while stirring constantly, for 2 minutes. Remove from heat and stir in the coconut oil. Divide between the serving bowls and top each portion with some freshly grated nutmeg.

Chocolate Mousse

YIELD: **4 SERVINGS**
PREP TIME: **5 MINUTES**
REFRIGERATION TIME: **1 HOUR**

NUTRITIONAL INFO:
(PER SERVING)
CALORIES: **239**
NET CARBS: **2 G**
CARBS: **6 G**
FAT: **22 G**
PROTEIN: **3 G**
FIBER: **4 G**

INGREDIENTS

1¾ OZ. 85 PERCENT DARK
CHOCOLATE, CHOPPED

1 TABLESPOON UNSALTED BUTTER

7 OZ. HEAVY CREAM

1 TEASPOON UNSWEETENED
COCOA POWDER

STEVIA OR PREFERRED KETO-
FRIENDLY SWEETENER, TO TASTE

DIRECTIONS

1. Place the chocolate and butter in a microwave-safe bowl and microwave for 30 seconds. Remove, stir to combine, and let cool.

2. Place the cream, cocoa powder, sweetener, and chocolate mixture in a mixing bowl and beat until soft peaks form.

3. Divide the mousse between serving bowls and refrigerate for at least an hour before serving.

Passion Fruit Mousse

YIELD: **4 SERVINGS**
PREP TIME: **5 MINUTES**
REFRIGERATION TIME: **4 HOURS**

NUTRITIONAL INFO:
(PER SERVING)
CALORIES: **354**
NET CARBS: **3.1 G**
CARBS: **4 G**
FAT: **35.1 G**
PROTEIN: **1 G**
FIBER: **0.9 G**

INGREDIENTS

2 PASSION FRUITS

8 OZ. MASCARPONE CHEESE,
AT ROOM TEMPERATURE

2 TABLESPOONS STEVIA OR
PREFERRED KETO-FRIENDLY
SWEETENER

½ TEASPOON PURE VANILLA
EXTRACT

2 TABLESPOONS WARM WATER
(110°F)

⅔ CUP HEAVY CREAM

DIRECTIONS

1. Scoop out the passion fruits' seeds and pulp into a small mixing bowl. Strain about half the pulp and juice into a mixing bowl. Add the mascarpone, sweetener, vanilla, and warm water to the bowl and beat the mixture until it is thick and smooth.

2. Place the cream in a separate mixing bowl and beat until it holds soft peaks. Working in three increments, fold the whipped cream into the passion fruit mixture. Divide the mousse between the serving dishes and top with the remaining passion fruit pulp and juice. Cover and refrigerate for 4 hours before serving.

Peanut Butter Mousse

YIELD: **8 SERVINGS**
PREP TIME: **15 MINUTES**
REFRIGERATION TIME: **30 MINUTES**

NUTRITIONAL INFO:
(PER SERVING)
CALORIES: **172**
NET CARBS: **2.3 G**
CARBS: **2.6 G**
FAT: **16.5 G**
PROTEIN: **5.2 G**
FIBER: **0.3 G**

INGREDIENTS

8.8 OZ. NATURAL, NO SUGAR ADDED PEANUT BUTTER

1 CUP GRANULATED ERYTHRITOL

8 OZ. CREAM CHEESE, AT ROOM TEMPERATURE

1 TEASPOON PURE VANILLA EXTRACT

¾ CUPS HEAVY CREAM

DIRECTIONS

1. Place the peanut butter and three-quarters of the erythritol in a mixing bowl and beat with a handheld mixer until light and fluffy. Add the cream cheese and vanilla and beat until incorporated.

2. Place the cream in a separate mixing bowl and beat until soft peaks form. Add the remaining erythritol, beat until incorporated, and then fold the whipped cream into the peanut butter mixture. Refrigerate for 30 minutes, or until slightly firm.

3. Remove the mousse from the refrigerator and beat with a handheld mixer until light and fluffy. Serve immediately or store in the refrigerator.

Brandied Pumpkin Mousse

YIELD: **10 SERVINGS**
PREP TIME: **15 MINUTES**
REFRIGERATION TIME: **1 HOUR**

NUTRITIONAL INFO:
(PER SERVING)
CALORIES: **200**
NET CARBS: **4.5 G**
CARBS: **5.9 G**
FAT: **17.9 G**
PROTEIN: **3.4 G**
FIBER: **1.4 G**

INGREDIENTS

12 OZ. CREAM CHEESE, AT ROOM TEMPERATURE

1 (14 OZ.) CAN OF PUMPKIN PUREE

½ CUP POWDERED ERYTHRITOL

3 TABLESPOONS BRANDY

1 TEASPOON PURE VANILLA EXTRACT

1½ TABLESPOONS PUMPKIN PIE SPICE, PLUS MORE FOR GARNISH

⅔ CUP HEAVY CREAM

DIRECTIONS

1. Place the cream cheese and pumpkin puree in a mixing bowl and beat with a handheld mixer until combined. Add the erythritol, brandy, vanilla, and pumpkin spice and beat until thoroughly combined. With the mixer running on high, gradually incorporate the cream and beat until the mixture is light and fluffy.

2. Scrape the mousse into the serving dishes and refrigerate for at least 1 hour before serving. To serve, sprinkle additional pumpkin pie spice on top of each portion.

Eton Mess

YIELD: **4 SERVINGS**
PREP TIME: **5 MINUTES**
COOKING TIME: **35 MINUTES**

NUTRITIONAL INFO:
(PER SERVING)
CALORIES: **146**
NET CARBS: **2 G**
CARBS: **3 G**
FAT: **14 G**
PROTEIN: **3 G**
FIBER: **1 G**

INGREDIENTS

2 EGG WHITES

¼ TEASPOON CREAM OF TARTAR

1 TEASPOON PURE VANILLA
EXTRACT

1½ TEASPOONS POWDERED
ERYTHRITOL

5⅓ OZ. HEAVY CREAM

STEVIA OR PREFERRED KETO-
FRIENDLY SWEETENER, TO TASTE

3½ OZ. STRAWBERRIES, HULLED
AND DICED

DIRECTIONS

1. Preheat the oven to 245°F and line a baking sheet with parchment paper. Place the egg whites in a bowl and beat until frothy. Add the cream of tartar and beat until soft peaks form. Add half of the vanilla and the erythritol and whisk to combine.

2. Transfer the mixture to the baking sheet and bake for 30 to 35 minutes, until cooked through. Remove and let the meringue cool for 15 minutes before removing from the parchment paper.

3. While the meringue is in the oven, place the heavy cream, sweetener, and the remaining vanilla in a bowl and beat until soft peaks form. Refrigerate for 15 minutes and then fold the strawberries into the mixture. Break the meringue into pieces, add it to the strawberries and cream, and serve.

Panna Cotta

YIELD: **3 SERVINGS**

PREP TIME: **5 MINUTES**

REFRIGERATION TIME: **4 HOURS**

NUTRITIONAL INFO:
(PER SERVING)

CALORIES: **204**

NET CARBS: **3 G**

CARBS: **3 G**

FAT: **20 G**

PROTEIN: **3 G**

FIBER: **0 G**

INGREDIENTS

1 TEASPOON GELATIN

2 TABLESPOONS WATER

½ CUP HEAVY CREAM

STEVIA OR PREFERRED KETO-FRIENDLY SWEETENER, TO TASTE

SEEDS AND POD FROM 1 VANILLA BEAN

MIXED BERRIES, FOR GARNISH

DIRECTIONS

1. Place the gelatin and the water in a mug and let the mixture sit for 5 minutes.

2. Pour the cream into a small saucepan and warm over low heat. Add the sweetener and stir until dissolved. Add the vanilla seeds and pod and stir to combine. When the cream comes to a simmer, remove the pan from heat and discard the vanilla pod. Add the gelatin mixture to the cream and stir until completely dissolved.

3. Pour the mixture into ramekins and chill in the refrigerator for at least 4 hours.

4. To unmold the panna cotta after they are set, dip the molds halfway into a bowl of hot water, then upend onto a plate. Top with mixed berries before serving.

Crème Brûlée

YIELD: **4 SERVINGS**
PREP TIME: **5 MINUTES**
REFRIGERATION TIME: **4 HOURS**

NUTRITIONAL INFO:
(PER SERVING)
CALORIES: **510**
NET CARBS: **8.9 G**
CARBS: **8.9 G**
FAT: **50.8 G**
PROTEIN: **6.5 G**
FIBER: **0 G**

INGREDIENTS

6 LARGE EGG YOLKS

¼ CUP STEVIA OR PREFERRED
KETO-FRIENDLY SWEETENER

2 CUPS HEAVY CREAM

1 TEASPOON PURE VANILLA
EXTRACT

1 TABLESPOON COGNAC

4 TEASPOONS SWERVE
CONFECTIONERS'

DIRECTIONS

1. Preheat the oven to 325°F, place four ramekins in a baking pan, and pour hot water into the pan until it is about halfway up the sides of the ramekins.

2. Place the egg yolks and 1 tablespoon of the sweetener in a mixing bowl and beat until pale and thick, about 3 minutes. Place the remaining sweetener and the cream in a saucepan and cook over medium heat, stirring occasionally, until bubbles start to appear around the edge. Remove from heat and gradually whisk in the egg yolk mixture. Stir in the vanilla and Cognac and divide the mixture between the ramekins.

3. Place in the oven and bake for about 25 minutes, until the custard is set at the edges and has a slight jiggle at the center. Remove from the oven, cover, and refrigerate for 4 hours.

4. To serve, sprinkle a teaspoon of the confectioners' sweetener over each serving and caramelize it with a kitchen torch.

Baked Coconut & Rum Custard

YIELD: **8 SERVINGS**
PREP TIME: **10 MINUTES**
REFRIGERATION TIME: **2 HOURS**

NUTRITIONAL INFO:
(PER SERVING)
CALORIES: **270**
NET CARBS: **2.7 G**
CARBS: **4.7 G**
FAT: **25.1 G**
PROTEIN: **4.9 G**
FIBER: **2 G**

INGREDIENTS

4 TABLESPOONS UNSALTED
BUTTER, MELTED AND COOLED

4 LARGE EGGS

1 CUP HEAVY CREAM

¾ CUP POWDERED ERYTHRITOL

½ CUP COCONUT MILK

3 TABLESPOONS RUM

2.6 OZ. UNSWEETENED SHREDDED
COCONUT

3 TABLESPOONS COCONUT FLOUR

½ TEASPOON BAKING POWDER

½ TEASPOON PURE VANILLA
EXTRACT

PINCH OF KOSHER SALT

DIRECTIONS

1. Preheat the oven to 350°F and grease a 9-inch pie plate with nonstick cooking spray. Place the butter, eggs, cream, erythritol, coconut milk, and rum in a blender and puree until combined. Add three-quarters of the coconut, the coconut flour, baking powder, vanilla, and salt and puree until combined.

2. Place the mixture in the pie plate and sprinkle the remaining coconut on top. Place in the oven and bake for about 45 minutes, until the edge is set and the center gives a slight wobble. Remove and let cool for 30 minutes at room temperature. Refrigerate for at least 2 hours before serving.

TIP: This custard can easily be transferred to a blind-baked piecrust or tart shell.

Raspberry Clafoutis

YIELD: **6 SERVINGS**
PREP TIME: **10 MINUTES**
COOKING TIME: **40 MINUTES**

NUTRITIONAL INFO:
(PER SERVING)
CALORIES: **145**
NET CARBS: **3.1 G**
CARBS: **6.7 G**
FAT: **11.9 G**
PROTEIN: **3.4 G**
FIBER: **3.6 G**

INGREDIENTS

2 TABLESPOONS UNSALTED
BUTTER, MELTED AND COOLED,
PLUS MORE AS NEEDED

2 LARGE EGGS

⅓ CUP HEAVY CREAM

¼ CUP COCONUT MILK

½ TEASPOON PURE VANILLA
EXTRACT

½ TEASPOON BAKING POWDER

⅓ CUP POWDERED ERYTHRITOL

3 TABLESPOONS COCONUT FLOUR

PINCH OF KOSHER SALT

6½ OZ. FRESH RASPBERRIES

DIRECTIONS

1. Preheat the oven to 350°F and grease a 9-inch pie plate with butter. Place the butter, eggs, cream, coconut milk, and vanilla in a mixing bowl and stir until thoroughly combined. Stir in all of the remaining ingredients, except for the raspberries, and work the mixture until it is a smooth batter.

2. Pour the batter into the pie plate and sprinkle the raspberries on top. Place in the oven and bake for about 40 minutes, until the edge is set and the center wobbles slightly. Remove from the oven and let the clafoutis set for about 25 minutes before serving.

NOTE: Don't hesitate to substitute your favorite fruit for the raspberries here. Part of the beauty of the clafoutis is how accommodating it is.

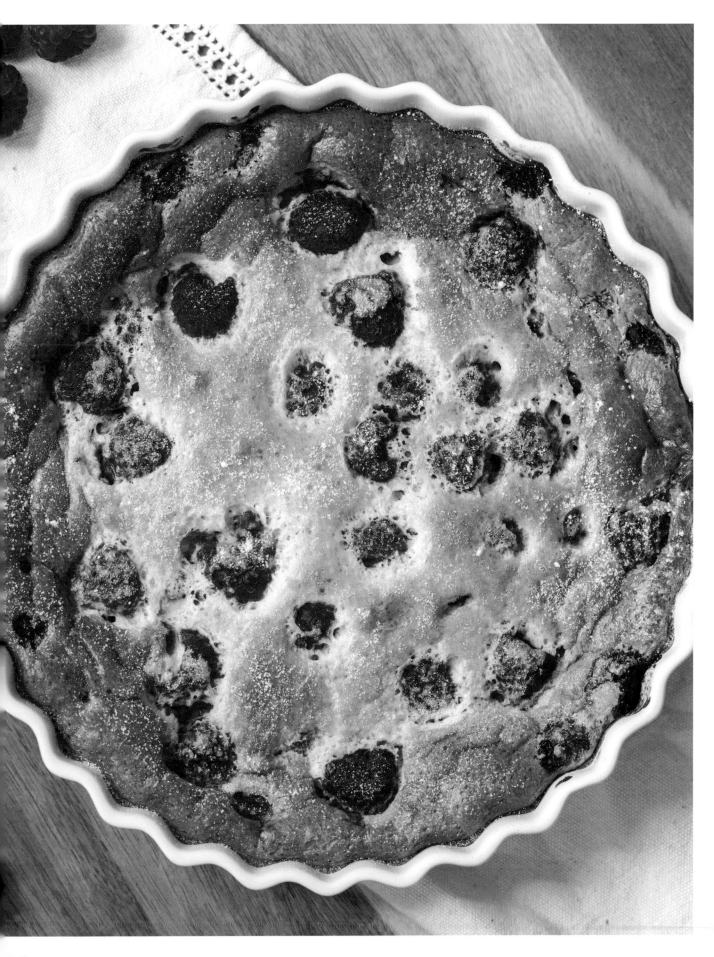

Pot de Crème

YIELD: **2 SERVINGS**
PREP TIME: **5 MINUTES**
COOKING TIME: **10 MINUTES**

NUTRITIONAL INFO:
(PER SERVING WITHOUT TOPPING)
CALORIES: **345**
NET CARBS: **6 G**
CARBS: **10 G**
FAT: **34 G**
PROTEIN: **5 G**
FIBER: **4 G**

INGREDIENTS

2.1 OZ. BAKER'S CHOCOLATE

1 EGG YOLK

2.8 OZ. HEAVY CREAM, PLUS MORE
AS NEEDED

1½ TEASPOONS POWDERED
ERYTHRITOL

2 TO 3 DROPS OF PURE VANILLA
EXTRACT

PINCH OF KOSHER SALT

CRÈME FRAÎCHE, FOR TOPPING
(OPTIONAL)

BERRY COMPOTE (SEE PAGE 23),
FOR TOPPING (OPTIONAL)

DIRECTIONS

1. Break the chocolate into small pieces and place them in a bowl. Place the egg yolk in a separate bowl and beat until scrambled.

2. Place the cream, erythritol, and vanilla in a saucepan and warm over low heat while stirring constantly. As soon as bubbles appear in the cream, remove the pan from heat. Add a spoonful of the hot cream to the egg yolk and whisk to combine. Stir the tempered yolk into the saucepan and cook the mixture over low heat until it is thick enough to coat the back of a wooden spoon.

3. Pour the custard over the chocolate, stir in the salt, and let the mixture sit for 1 minute. Whisk until the mixture is a thick pudding and, if desired, top with crème fraîche or berry compote.

Tiramisu

YIELD: **8 SERVINGS**
PREP TIME: **10 MINUTES**
REFRIGERATION TIME: **10 MINUTES**

NUTRITIONAL INFO:
(PER SERVING)
CALORIES: **308**
NET CARBS: **5 G**
CARBS: **6 G**
FAT: **29 G**
PROTEIN: **16 G**
FIBER: **1 G**

INGREDIENTS

2.1 OZ. BREWED ESPRESSO

2 TABLESPOONS WHISKEY
(OPTIONAL)

2 TABLESPOONS HEAVY CREAM

1 EGG, YOLK AND WHITE
SEPARATED

STEVIA OR PREFERRED KETO-
FRIENDLY SWEETENER, TO TASTE

14 OZ. MASCARPONE CHEESE

2 PORTIONS OF MUG BREAD
(SEE SIDEBAR)

2 TEASPOONS UNSWEETENED
COCOA POWDER

DIRECTIONS

1. Place the espresso, whiskey, and cream in a bowl and stir to combine. Place the egg white in a bowl and whisk until stiff peaks form. Set aside.

2. Place the egg yolk and sweetener in a separate bowl and whisk until the mixture is a pale yellow. Add the mascarpone cheese and 2.1 oz. of the espresso mixture and whisk until it becomes a smooth custard. Working in two batches, fold in the beaten egg white.

3. Slice the bread as desired and then dip the slices into the remaining espresso mixture. Layer them in the dish, pour the custard over the top, and refrigerate until set, about 10 minutes. Dust with the cocoa powder before serving.

MUG BREAD

Place 1 oz. almond flour, 1 tablespoon olive oil, ½ teaspoon baking powder, and 1 egg in a large mug and stir to combine. Place the mug in the microwave and microwave on medium for 1½ minutes. Remove, turn the mug over, and tap it until the bread slides out. This recipe will produce 1 serving. The macros per serving are as follows: 324 calories, 2 grams net carbs, 5 grams carbs, 28 grams fat, 13 grams protein, 3 grams fiber.

Chocolate Soufflés

YIELD: **4 SERVINGS**
PREP TIME: **5 MINUTES**
COOKING TIME: **30 MINUTES**

NUTRITIONAL INFO:
(PER SERVING)
CALORIES: **166**
NET CARBS: **3.9 G**
CARBS: **6 G**
FAT: **13.9 G**
PROTEIN: **7.9 G**
FIBER: **2.1 G**

INGREDIENTS

1 TABLESPOON UNSALTED BUTTER, AT ROOM TEMPERATURE

1¾ OZ. BAKER'S CHOCOLATE OR SUGAR-FREE CHOCOLATE CHIPS

¼ CUP STEVIA OR PREFERRED KETO-FRIENDLY SWEETENER, PLUS 2 TEASPOONS

4 LARGE EGGS, YOLKS AND WHITES SEPARATED

½ TEASPOON PURE VANILLA EXTRACT

PINCH OF CREAM OF TARTAR

PINCH OF SEA SALT

DIRECTIONS

1. Preheat the oven to 375°F and grease four ramekins with the butter. Place them on a baking sheet.

2. Place the chocolate in a microwave-safe bowl and microwave on medium until melted, removing to stir every 10 seconds.

3. Place the sweetener and egg yolks in a mixing bowl and beat with a handheld mixer until the mixture is pale and thick. Fold in the melted chocolate and vanilla and then wipe off the beaters.

4. Place the egg whites in a mixing bowl and beat until frothy. Add the cream of tartar and salt beat on high until moist, stiff peaks form. Stir one-third of the whipped egg whites into the chocolate mixture. Gently fold the remaining egg whites into the chocolate mixture and then divide the mixture between the ramekins.

5. Place in the oven and bake for 11 to 15 minutes, until the soufflés are set at their edges, but their interiors are still creamy. Remove from the oven and serve immediately.

Cheesecake Parfaits

YIELD: **6 SERVINGS**
PREP TIME: **15 MINUTES**
REFRIGERATION TIME: **15 MINUTES**

NUTRITIONAL INFO:
(PER SERVING)
CALORIES: **239**
NET CARBS: **3.8 G**
CARBS: **4.2 G**
FAT: **22.9 G**
PROTEIN: **4.1 G**
FIBER: **0.4 G**

INGREDIENTS

8 OZ. CREAM CHEESE, AT ROOM
TEMPERATURE

⅔ CUP HEAVY CREAM

⅓ CUP POWDERED ERYTHRITOL

2 TABLESPOONS GRAND MARNIER

2 TEASPOONS ORANGE ZEST

4 OZ. FRESH STRAWBERRIES,
HULLED AND DICED

DIRECTIONS

1. Place all of the ingredients, except for the strawberries, in a mixing bowl and beat with a handheld mixer until light and fluffy.

2. Spoon half of the mixture into six serving dishes. Top with half of the strawberries, and then repeat with remaining cheese and strawberries. Refrigerate for 15 minutes before serving.

Mocha & Chia Seed Parfaits

YIELD: **6 SERVINGS**

PREP TIME: **5 MINUTES**

REFRIGERATION TIME: **24 HOURS**

NUTRITIONAL INFO:
(PER SERVING)

CALORIES: **183**

NET CARBS: **6.9 G**

CARBS: **19.6 G**

FAT: **11 G**

PROTEIN: **7.5 G**

FIBER: **12.7 G**

INGREDIENTS

5⅔ OZ. CHIA SEEDS

2½ CUPS UNSWEETENED ALMOND MILK

1 CUP ALMOND MILK YOGURT

1 TABLESPOON STEVIA OR PREFERRED KETO-FRIENDLY SWEETENER

¼ CUP CACAO OR UNSWEETENED COCOA POWDER

¼ CUP BREWED ESPRESSO, AT ROOM TEMPERATURE

DIRECTIONS

1. Place the chia seeds, almond milk, yogurt, and sweetener in a mixing bowl and stir to combine. Cover with plastic wrap and let stand at room temperature for 30 minutes.

2. Stir the mixture again, sift the cacao or cocoa powder over it, add the espresso, and stir to combine. Divide between the serving dishes, cover with plastic wrap, and refrigerate overnight.

Chocolate & Chia Parfaits

YIELD: **4 SERVINGS**
PREP TIME: **5 MINUTES**
REFRIGERATION TIME: **24 HOURS**

NUTRITIONAL INFO:
(PER SERVING)
CALORIES: **296**
NET CARBS: **7.2 G**
CARBS: **28.7 G**
FAT: **18.5 G**
PROTEIN: **12.9 G**
FIBER: **21.5 G**

INGREDIENTS

5⅔ OZ. CHIA SEEDS

2½ CUPS UNSWEETENED ALMOND MILK

2 TABLESPOONS STEVIA OR PREFERRED KETO-FRIENDLY SWEETENER

1.2 OZ. UNSWEETENED CACAO POWDER

¼ CUP PLAIN GREEK YOGURT

0.8 OZ. BLUEBERRIES

1 OZ. BLACKBERRIES

1 TABLESPOON CHOPPED SUGAR-FREE BITTERSWEET CHOCOLATE

DIRECTIONS

1. Place the chia seeds, almond milk, and sweetener in a mixing bowl and stir to combine. Cover the bowl and let the mixture stand at room temperature for 30 minutes.

2. Stir the mixture and then sift the cacao powder over it, while stirring constantly. Divide the mixture between four serving glasses, cover, and refrigerate overnight.

3. Top each portion with some of the yogurt, berries, and chocolate.

Orange, Chia & Pistachio Parfaits

YIELD: **4 SERVINGS**
PREP TIME: **5 MINUTES**
REFRIGERATION TIME: **24 HOURS**

NUTRITIONAL INFO:
(PER SERVING)
CALORIES: **358**
NET CARBS: **4.9 G**
CARBS: **17.5 G**
FAT: **29.7 G**
PROTEIN: **12.1 G**
FIBER: **12.6 G**

INGREDIENTS

2 CUPS COCONUT MILK

2 CUPS UNSWEETENED ALMOND MILK

1.4 OZ. WHITE CHIA SEEDS

1.4 OZ. BLACK CHIA SEEDS

1 TABLESPOON STEVIA OR PREFERRED KETO-FRIENDLY SWEETENER

½ TEASPOON ORANGE BLOSSOM WATER

JUICE OF ½ ORANGE

1¾ OZ. UNSALTED PISTACHIOS, CHOPPED

DIRECTIONS

1. Place the coconut milk, almond milk, chia seeds, sweetener, and orange blossom water in a mixing bowl and stir to combine. Cover and refrigerate overnight.

2. Stir the orange juice into the pudding. Divide between the serving bowls and sprinkle some of the pistachios on top of each portion.

TIP: This pudding will also work for breakfast if you're looking for a sweeter start to the day.

Golden Milk

YIELD: **2 SERVINGS**
PREP TIME: **5 MINUTES**
COOKING TIME: **10 MINUTES**

NUTRITIONAL INFO:
(PER SERVING)
CALORIES: **50**
NET CARBS: **2 G**
CARBS: **3.9 G**
FAT: **4.6 G**
PROTEIN: **1.5 G**
FIBER: **1.9 G**

INGREDIENTS

2⅓ CUPS UNSWEETENED ALMOND MILK

2 TEASPOONS PEELED AND GRATED FRESH TURMERIC ROOT

1 TEASPOON GROUND TURMERIC, PLUS MORE FOR GARNISH

⅛ TEASPOON GROUND GINGER

⅛ TEASPOON CINNAMON

3 CARDAMOM PODS, LIGHTLY CRUSHED

1 TEASPOON STEVIA OR PREFERRED KETO-FRIENDLY SWEETENER

DIRECTIONS

1. Place ¼ cup of the almond milk, the turmeric root, ground turmeric, ground ginger, cinnamon, and cardamom pods in a saucepan and warm over medium heat, whisking occasionally, until a smooth paste forms.

2. Whisk in 1¾ cups of the almond milk while pouring in a slow, steady stream. Bring to a simmer and cook until the mixture is warmed through but not boiling, 3 to 4 minutes. Strain the milk into the serving glasses and stir some of the sweetener into each.

3. Pour the remaining almond milk into a small saucepan and bring it to a simmer over medium heat. Froth it with a milk frother and spoon some on top of each beverage. Dust with additional turmeric and serve.

WHIPPED CREAM

Place 2 cups heavy cream and 1 teaspoon pure vanilla extract in a mixing bowl and beat until soft peaks form. Use immediately or store in the refrigerator, where it will keep for up to 3 days. This preparation will produce 12 servings (4 cups) of whipped cream. The macros per serving are as follows: 138 calories, 1.2 grams net carbs, 1.2 grams carbs, 14.7 grams fat, 0.8 grams protein, 0 grams fiber.

Café Mocha

YIELD: **8 SERVINGS**
PREP TIME: **5 MINUTES**
COOKING TIME: **5 MINUTES**

NUTRITIONAL INFO:
(PER SERVING)
CALORIES: **283**
NET CARBS: **8.4 G**
CARBS: **10.5 G**
FAT: **26.5 G**
PROTEIN: **6 G**
FIBER: **2.1 G**

INGREDIENTS

3½ CUPS WHOLE MILK

1 CUP HEAVY CREAM

½ CUP BREWED ESPRESSO

⅓ CUP STEVIA OR PREFERRED
KETO-FRIENDLY SWEETENER

4 OZ. BAKER'S CHOCOLATE,
GRATED

2 TEASPOONS ORANGE ZEST

½ TEASPOON FLAKY SEA SALT

1 CUP WHIPPED CREAM
(SEE SIDEBAR)

DIRECTIONS

1. Place the milk, cream, and espresso in a saucepan and warm over medium heat. Stir in the sweetener and continue stirring until it has dissolved.

2. Set 1 tablespoon of the chocolate aside and place the rest in a bowl. When the espresso mixture is hot, ladle 1 cup at a time into the bowl containing the chocolate and whisk until all of it has been incorporated and the chocolate is completely melted.

3. Stir in the orange zest and salt, pour into warmed mugs, and top each serving with some of the reserved chocolate and the Whipped Cream.

Mexican Hot Chocolate

YIELD: **8 SERVINGS**
PREP TIME: **5 MINUTES**
COOKING TIME: **10 MINUTES**

NUTRITIONAL INFO:
(PER SERVING)
CALORIES: **262**
NET CARBS: **7 G**
CARBS: **9.9 G**
FAT: **25.4 G**
PROTEIN: **5 G**
FIBER: **2.9 G**

INGREDIENTS

2 CUPS WHOLE MILK

1 CUP HEAVY CREAM

3 CINNAMON STICKS

1 RED CHILI PEPPER, PIERCED

⅓ CUP STEVIA OR PREFERRED
KETO-FRIENDLY SWEETENER

¼ CUP UNSWEETENED COCOA
POWDER

4 OZ. BAKER'S CHOCOLATE,
GRATED

1 TEASPOON PURE VANILLA
EXTRACT

¾ TEASPOON GRATED FRESH
NUTMEG

½ TEASPOON FLAKY SEA SALT

1 CUP WHIPPED CREAM
(SEE PAGE 238)

½ TEASPOON RED PEPPER FLAKES
(OPTIONAL)

DIRECTIONS

1. Place the milk, cream, cinnamon sticks, and chili pepper in a saucepan and warm over medium-low heat for 5 to 6 minutes, making sure the mixture does not come to a boil. Remove the pan from heat and discard the cinnamon sticks and chili pepper.

2. Place the sweetener and cocoa powder in a small bowl and whisk to combine. Gradually whisk in about 1 cup of the mixture in the saucepan and then pour the resulting mixture into the saucepan.

3. Add the chocolate, reduce the heat to low, and cook, whisking constantly, until the chocolate has melted. Whisk in the vanilla, nutmeg, and salt, ladle into warmed mugs, and top with the Whipped Cream and red pepper flakes (if desired).

CHAPTER 6

BLISSFUL

BITES

A select company of small treats with outsized flavors. From the impossibly effortless bliss balls that started as a keto staple before becoming favorites in all corners of the wellness community, to a host of the decadent truffles, the only issue with these desserts is training your mind not to feel guilty while you're enjoying them.

Chia & Sesame Bliss Balls

YIELD: **12 SERVINGS**
PREP TIME: **5 MINUTES**
FREEZING TIME: **20 MINUTES**

NUTRITIONAL INFO:
(PER SERVING)
CALORIES: **199**
NET CARBS: **1.5 G**
CARBS: **7.1 G**
FAT: **18.9 G**
PROTEIN: **3 G**
FIBER: **5.6 G**

INGREDIENTS

½ CUP COCONUT OIL, MELTED

½ CUP COCONUT BUTTER, MELTED

¼ CUP CACAO POWDER

1 TEASPOON PURE ALMOND
EXTRACT

½ TEASPOON PURE VANILLA
EXTRACT

½ TEASPOON LIQUID STEVIA
OR PREFERRED KETO-FRIENDLY
SWEETENER

2.8 OZ. WHITE CHIA SEEDS

2 TABLESPOONS SESAME SEEDS

DIRECTIONS

1. Place the coconut oil and coconut butter in a bowl and stir to combine. Stir in the cacao powder, extracts, and sweetener, cover the bowl, and freeze until the mixture is set, about 20 minutes.

2. Combine the chia seeds and sesame seeds in a shallow bowl. Form 2-tablespoon portions of the mixture into balls and roll them in the seed mixture. Serve immediately or store in the refrigerator.

Coconut Bliss Balls

YIELD: **12 SERVINGS**
PREP TIME: **5 MINUTES**
FREEZING TIME: **20 MINUTES**

NUTRITIONAL INFO:
(PER SERVING)
CALORIES: **212**
NET CARBS: **4.3 G**
CARBS: **6.5 G**
FAT: **20.7 G**
PROTEIN: **3 G**
FIBER: **2.2 G**

INGREDIENTS

½ CUP COCONUT OIL, MELTED

½ CUP NO SUGAR ADDED ALMOND
BUTTER, MELTED

2 TABLESPOONS REAL MAPLE SYRUP

3.2 OZ. UNSWEETENED SHREDDED
COCONUT

1¾ OZ. ALMONDS, CHOPPED

½ TEASPOON PURE VANILLA
EXTRACT

PINCH OF KOSHER SALT

DIRECTIONS

1. Place the coconut oil, almond butter, and maple syrup
    in a bowl and stir to combine. Stir in two-thirds of the
    coconut, the almonds, vanilla, and salt, cover the bowl,
    and freeze until set, about 20 minutes.

2. Place the remaining coconut in a shallow bowl. Form
    2-tablespoon portions of the mixture into balls and roll
    them in the coconut. Serve immediately or store in the
    refrigerator.

Pistachio Bliss Balls

YIELD: **12 SERVINGS**
PREP TIME: **5 MINUTES**
FREEZING TIME: **20 MINUTES**

NUTRITIONAL INFO:
(PER SERVING)
CALORIES: **218**
NET CARBS: **4.7 G**
CARBS: **7.7 G**
FAT: **19.5 G**
PROTEIN: **5.2 G**
FIBER: **3 G**

INGREDIENTS

½ CUP COCONUT OIL

4.4 OZ. NATURAL, NO SUGAR
ADDED PEANUT BUTTER

¼ CUP CACAO POWDER

1 TEASPOON LIQUID STEVIA OR
PREFERRED KETO-FRIENDLY
SWEETENER

PINCH OF KOSHER SALT

1 TABLESPOON DRIED
CRANBERRIES, MINCED

2.7 OZ. PISTACHIO MEATS,
CHOPPED

DIRECTIONS

1. Place the coconut oil and peanut butter in a microwave-safe bowl and microwave on medium until melted, removing to stir every 15 seconds. Stir in all of the remaining ingredients other than the pistachios, cover the bowl, and freeze until set, about 20 minutes.

2. Place the chopped pistachios in a shallow bowl. Form 2-tablespoon portions of the mixture into balls and roll them in the nuts. Serve immediately or store in the refrigerator.

Avocado & Chocolate Truffles

YIELD: **36 TRUFFLES**
(1 SERVING = 2 TRUFFLES)
PREP TIME: **5 MINUTES**
REFRIGERATION TIME: **30 MINUTES**

NUTRITIONAL INFO:
(PER SERVING)
CALORIES: **115**
NET CARBS: **9.7 G**
CARBS: **12.6 G**
FAT: **8.2 G**
PROTEIN: **0.7 G**
FIBER: **2.9 G**

INGREDIENTS

12.4 OZ. SUGAR-FREE SEMISWEET
CHOCOLATE CHIPS

FLESH OF 2 AVOCADOS

2 TEASPOONS PURE VANILLA
EXTRACT

½ TEASPOON KOSHER SALT

STEVIA OR PREFERRED KETO-
FRIENDLY SWEETENER, TO TASTE

½ CUP UNSWEETENED COCOA
POWDER

DIRECTIONS

1. Place the chocolate chips in a microwave-safe bowl and microwave on medium until melted, removing to stir every 10 seconds.

2. Place the avocados, vanilla, and salt in a bowl and stir to combine. Fold in the melted chocolate and then stir in the sweetener. Cover the bowl and refrigerate for 30 minutes.

3. Place the cocoa powder in a shallow bowl. Form approximately ¾-tablespoon portions of the mixture into balls, roll them in the cocoa powder, and serve.

Chocolate & Almond Truffles

YIELD: **32 TRUFFLES**
(1 SERVING = 2 TRUFFLES)

PREP TIME: **5 MINUTES**

REFRIGERATION TIME: **2 HOURS AND 30 MINUTES**

NUTRITIONAL INFO:
(PER SERVING)

CALORIES: **158**

NET CARBS: **7 G**

CARBS: **8.6 G**

FAT: **14.1 G**

PROTEIN: **2.3 G**

FIBER: **1.6 G**

INGREDIENTS

5½ OZ. SUGAR-FREE BITTERSWEET CHOCOLATE CHIPS

4 TABLESPOONS UNSALTED BUTTER

⅔ CUP HEAVY CREAM

1 TEASPOON PURE ALMOND EXTRACT

1½ CUPS CHOPPED ALMONDS

DIRECTIONS

1. Place the chocolate chips, butter, and cream in a heatproof bowl. Set it over a saucepan half-full of simmering water and stir until the mixture is melted and smooth. Remove from heat and stir in the almond extract. Let the mixture cool for 5 minutes. Cover with plastic wrap and refrigerate for 2 hours.

2. Line a large baking sheet with parchment paper. Form generous teaspoons of the mixture into balls and place them on the baking sheet. Cover with plastic wrap and refrigerate for 30 minutes.

3. Place the almonds in a shallow bowl and roll the truffles in them before serving.

Chocolate & Peanut Butter Truffles

YIELD: **32 TRUFFLES**
(1 SERVING = 2 TRUFFLES)
PREP TIME: **10 MINUTES**
REFRIGERATION TIME: **2 HOURS**

NUTRITIONAL INFO:
(PER SERVING)
CALORIES: **212**
NET CARBS: **8.8 G**
CARBS: **9.9 G**
FAT: **20.4 G**
PROTEIN: **2.3 G**
FIBER: **1.1 G**

INGREDIENTS

2½ OZ. SUGAR-FREE WHITE
CHOCOLATE CHIPS

¾ CUP COCONUT OIL

8 OZ. CRUNCHY, NO SUGAR ADDED
PEANUT BUTTER

⅓ CUP HEAVY CREAM

2 TEASPOONS STEVIA OR
PREFERRED KETO-FRIENDLY
SWEETENER

6¼ OZ. SUGAR-FREE BITTERSWEET
CHOCOLATE CHIPS

DIRECTIONS

1. Place the white chocolate chips, ½ cup of the coconut oil, the peanut butter, and cream in a heatproof bowl and stir to combine. Place the bowl over a half-full saucepan of simmering water and stir until the mixture is smooth and combined. Remove from heat, stir in the sweetener, cover with plastic wrap, and refrigerate for 2 hours.

2. Line a large baking sheet with parchment paper. Form generous teaspoons of the mixture into balls, place them on the baking sheet, and freeze for 1 hour.

3. Place the bittersweet chocolate chips and the remaining coconut oil in a microwave-safe bowl and microwave on medium until melted, removing to stir every 10 seconds. Using a fork or skewer, dip the truffles in the melted chocolate, shaking off any excess. Return to the baking sheet and let sit at room temperature until the chocolate has set, about 1 hour.

Cashew & Coconut Truffles

YIELD: **24 TRUFFLES**
(1 SERVING = 2 TRUFFLES)
PREP TIME: **5 MINUTES**
REFRIGERATION TIME: **1 HOUR**

NUTRITIONAL INFO:
(PER SERVING)
CALORIES: **266**
NET CARBS: **3.6 G**
CARBS: **7.7 G**
FAT: **25 G**
PROTEIN: **4.7 G**
FIBER: **4.1 G**

INGREDIENTS

2.6 OZ. RAW CASHEWS

¼ CUP COCONUT FLOUR

⅓ CUP CACAO OR UNSWEETENED COCOA POWDER

½ TEASPOON TURMERIC

⅛ TEASPOON CINNAMON

¾ CUP COCONUT OIL

¾ CUP NO SUGAR ADDED ALMOND BUTTER

½ TEASPOON LIQUID STEVIA

2 OZ. UNSWEETENED SHREDDED COCONUT

DIRECTIONS

1. Place the cashews in a food processor and pulse until very finely chopped. Transfer the cashews to a mixing bowl and stir in the coconut flour, cacao or cocoa powder, turmeric, and cinnamon. Set the mixture aside.

2. Place the coconut oil, almond butter, and sweetener in a saucepan and melt over medium heat, while stirring occasionally. Pour the mixture into the cashew mixture and stir until thoroughly combined. Cover the bowl with plastic wrap and refrigerate for 30 minutes.

3. Place the coconut in a shallow bowl. Form scant tablespoons of the mixture into balls, roll them in the shredded coconut, and place the truffles on a parchment-lined baking sheet. Cover with plastic wrap and refrigerate for 30 minutes before serving.

Hazelnut Balls

YIELD: **18 SERVINGS**
PREP TIME: **5 MINUTES**
COOKING TIME: **1 HOUR**

NUTRITIONAL INFO:
(PER SERVING)
CALORIES: **214**
NET CARBS: **8.3 G**
CARBS: **14.5 G**
FAT: **19.4 G**
PROTEIN: **4.7 G**
FIBER: **6.2 G**

INGREDIENTS

1⅔ OZ. SUGAR-FREE SEMISWEET CHOCOLATE CHIPS

5 LARGE EGGS, YOLKS AND WHITES SEPARATED

½ CUP STEVIA OR PREFERRED KETO-FRIENDLY SWEETENER, PLUS MORE TO TASTE

5 OZ. HAZELNUTS, FINELY GROUND

PINCH OF KOSHER SALT

1 CUP CHOCOLATE FROSTING (SEE PAGE 65)

7½ OZ. SUGAR-FREE BITTERSWEET CHOCOLATE CHIPS

½ CUP HEAVY CREAM

DIRECTIONS

1. Preheat the oven to 350°F and line a springform pan with parchment paper. Place the semisweet chocolate chips in a microwave-safe bowl and microwave on medium until melted, removing to stir every 15 seconds.

2. Place the egg yolks and sweetener in a mixing bowl and beat with a handheld mixer until pale and very thick. Stir in the melted chocolate and then fold in the ground hazelnuts.

3. Place the egg whites and salt in a separate mixing bowl and beat until the mixture holds stiff peaks. Working in three increments, fold the mixture into the hazelnut mixture.

4. Scrape the batter into the pan, place it in the oven, and bake for about 25 minutes, until the cake is dry to the touch. Remove and let cool completely on a wire rack.

5. Cut the cake into pieces and add them to a food processor in batches. Pulse until they are crumbs and then place the crumbs in a mixing bowl. Stir in the frosting until you are able to form the mixture into balls; you may not need to use all of the frosting. Form the mixture into golf ball–sized spheres, place them on a parchment-lined baking sheet, and store them in the freezer.

6. Place the bittersweet chocolate chips in a heatproof bowl. Warm the cream in a saucepan until it is just about to come to a boil. Pour the cream over the chocolate, let stand for 1 minute, and then stir until smooth.

7. Let the mixture cool for 5 minutes and remove the balls from the freezer. Dip them into the chocolate until completely coated, place them back on the baking sheet, and freeze until the chocolate has set, about 15 minutes.

Vegan Chocolate Candies

YIELD: **24 CANDIES**
(1 SERVING = 2 CANDIES)
PREP TIME: **5 MINUTES**
REFRIGERATION TIME: **1 HOUR**

NUTRITIONAL INFO:
(PER SERVING)
CALORIES: **131**
NET CARBS: **8.5 G**
CARBS: **10.1 G**
FAT: **10.5 G**
PROTEIN: **2 G**
FIBER: **1.6 G**

INGREDIENTS

2 TABLESPOONS ACAI BERRIES

2 TABLESPOONS HEMP HEARTS

½ CUP COCONUT MILK

1 TEASPOON WHEATGRASS POWDER

2 TABLESPOONS STEVIA OR
PREFERRED KETO-FRIENDLY
SWEETENER

5 OZ. SUGAR-FREE BITTERSWEET
CHOCOLATE CHIPS

¼ CUP COCONUT OIL

2 TABLESPOONS CAROB POWDER

DIRECTIONS

1. Place the berries, hemp hearts, coconut milk, wheatgrass powder, and sweetener in a food processor and let the mixture stand for 10 minutes. Puree until smooth, pour the mixture into a heatproof bowl, and stir in the chocolate chips, coconut oil, and carob powder.

2. Place the bowl over a half-full saucepan of simmering water and stir occasionally until the chocolate has melted and the mixture is smooth.

3. Spray a candy mold with nonstick cooking spray. Pour the chocolate mixture into the molds and refrigerate for 1 hour before serving.

METRIC CONVERSIONS

U.S. Measurement	Approximate Metric Liquid Measurement	Approximate Metric Dry Measurement
1 teaspoon	5 ml	5 g
1 tablespoon or ½ ounce	15 ml	14 g
1 ounce or ⅛ cup	30 ml	29 g
¼ cup or 2 ounces	60 ml	57 g
⅓ cup	80 ml	76 g
½ cup or 4 ounces	120 ml	113 g
⅔ cup	160 ml	151 g
¾ cup or 6 ounces	180 ml	170 g
1 cup or 8 ounces or ½ pint	240 ml	227 g
1½ cups or 12 ounces	350 ml	340 g
2 cups or 1 pint or 16 ounces	475 ml	454 g
3 cups or 1½ pints	700 ml	680 g
4 cups or 2 pints or 1 quart	950 ml	908 g

INDEX

ABOUT CIDER MILL PRESS
BOOK PUBLISHERS

❋ ❋ ❋

Good ideas ripen with time. From seed to harvest, Cider Mill Press brings fine reading, information, and entertainment together between the covers of its creatively crafted books. Our Cider Mill bears fruit twice a year, publishing a new crop of titles each spring and fall.

"Where Good Books Are Ready for Press"

Visit us online at
www.cidermillpress.com
or write to us at
PO Box 454
12 Spring St.
Kennebunkport, Maine 04046